Sandra Lee

semi-homemade

Money Saving
Slow Cooking

This book belongs to:

_____

Solution-based

Enterprise that

Motivates,

Inspires, and

Helps

Organize and

Manage time, while

Enriching

Modern life by

Adding

Dependable shortcuts

Every day.

Published by John Wiley & Sons, Inc., Hoboken, New Jersey, in partnership with SL Books.

Published simultaneously in Canada.

Cover photo by George Lange; selected author photos by Jill Lotenberg.

For general information on our other products and services or for technical support, please contact our Customer Care Department within the United States at (800) 762-2974, outside the United States at (317) 572-3993 or fax (317) 572-4002.

Wiley also publishes its books in a variety of electronic formats. Some content that appears in print may not be available in electronic books. For more information about Wiley products, visit our web site at www.wiley.com.

Library of Congress Cataloging-in-Publication Data:
Lee, Sandra, 1966-
  Sandra Lee semi-homemade money saving slow cooking : 129 quick-to-cook meals.
      p. cm.
  Includes index.
  ISBN 978-0-470-54026-8
  1. Electric cookery, Slow. 2. Quick and easy cookery. 3. Brand name products—United States. 4. Low budget cookery. I. Title.
  TX827.L42 2009
  641.5'884--dc22

                                                    2009029984

Printed in the United States of America.

10 9 8 7 6 5 4 3 2 1

 **SL BOOKS**
sandralee.com

 **WILEY**
John Wiley & Sons, Inc.

sem·i-home·made

adj. 1: a stress-free solution-based formula that provides savvy shortcuts and affordable, timesaving tips for overextended do-it-yourself homemakers **2:** a quick and easy equation wherein 70% ready-made convenience products are added to 30% fresh ingredients with creative personal style, allowing homemakers to take 100% of the credit for something that looks, feels, or tastes homemade **3:** a foolproof resource for having it all—and having the time to enjoy it **4:** a method created by Sandra Lee for home, garden, crafts, beauty, food, fashion, and entertaining wherein everything looks, tastes, and feels as if it was made from scratch.

Table of Contents

Chapter 1

Everyday
Finger Foods
18

Chapter 3

Gatherings and
Get-Togethers
56

Chapter 2

Meals in a Bowl
34

Chapter 4

Desserts
78

Dedication

To Grandma Lorraine, for all the loving days and delicious dishes.

Letter from Sandra

Frugal-friendly. Cost-conscious. Budget-based. These are the watchwords of today. Time and money are treasured things we long for but find in increasingly short supply. Thrifty at heart, I'm always looking for ways to stretch every dollar—and every hour—in real life and on my Food Network shows, *Sandra's Money Saving Meals* and *Semi-Homemade Cooking*.

When it comes to convenience, the slow cooker is the best bargain around. This amazing appliance is a modern must-have, an undemanding helper that cooks all day while you work or play. Toss in a chicken or a roast in the morning, push the button, and go—then come home to a "dinner's ready" aroma that greets you like a warm hug.

Slow cooking is a lot slower if you have to chop vegetables, brown meat, and dirty a sink full of dishes for mixing and measuring. While other recipes have ingredients that go on and on, my timesaving shortcuts cut the prep work with a short list of inexpensive ready-to-go meats, all-in-one seasonings, and prepared soups and stocks—all are already-on-hand ingredients that add a complexity of flavor with a simplicity of effort.

For more money saving recipes, tips, and ideas, log onto www.semihomemade.com. Join my magazine family there too!

It's the cornerstone of my "Triple A Factor"—creating meals that are Accessible and Aspirational, yet still Affordable. Slow cooking is stress-free, simmering in home-cooked flavor all day—yet the time you invest is minimal. Electricity costs around two cents per hour—far less than a stove—and you can save even more by using tough, inexpensive cuts of meat that cook up fall-off-the-fork tender in rich, velvety juices just begging for bread for dunking.

Cook for one, feed the entire family, or be the hit of the holiday season. *Money Saving Slow Cooking* gives everyone a head start on a wholesome dinner with 129 brand-new, easy recipes that cover all the basics from make-ahead meals to potluck parties. There are hearty dishes, lighter fare, cozy comfort food, and family favorites roasted, steamed, and braised to bubbly perfection. Meaty stews, homey casseroles, and one-pot pastas pair with bagged salad greens to make incredible meals that are ready whenever you are.

Main dishes, finger foods, hot toddies, and desserts—anything goes in a slow cooker. Plug in to your own money saving meals and have a wealth of good food at your fingertips. The slow cooker does the work while you relish every bite.

Cheers to a happy, healthy home,

Sandra Lee

Pork Shoulder

Cut-Up
Whole Chicken

Meat: A Cut Above

It is a happy coincidence that the most flavorful cuts of meat are also the least expensive. They simply require a low, slow, and moist cooking method to bring out their best—which just happens to be how the slow cooker cooks. The following cuts are easy on the pocketbook and perfect for the slow cooker.

Pork Shoulder: This is the cut used for classic Southern-style pulled pork. It's also delicious flavored with Mexican seasonings and spices, then shredded and eaten drizzled with pan juices in tortillas with fresh pico de gallo, salsa, or crunchy shredded cabbage and chopped radishes. Various versions of it are called blade roast or Boston butt. It comes both bone-in and boneless.

Beef Cuts: The most economical cuts of beef come from two areas on the animal: the chuck, which is the shoulder and upper back, and the round, which is essentially the rear of the animal. Both these areas get the most exercise and are therefore the toughest—but also the tastiest. Most pot roasts and short ribs come from the chuck; bottom and top round roast, rump roast, and eye round roast come from the round.

Chicken: Buying a whole chicken—cut up or left whole—is the most budget-minded way to enjoy America's favorite bird. Because it comes bone-in and skin-on, it cooks up juicy and flavorful in the slow cooker and doesn't dry out.

Bread and Butter
Pot Roast

Beef Chuck Roast

Bottom Round Roast

Chuck 7-Bone
Pot Roast

Chuck Short Ribs

Beef on a Budget
Despite its reputation as a bit of a luxury, beef serves up rich flavor your family can enjoy each week without breaking the bank. All the inexpensive cuts shown here are perfect for your slow cooker.

Flavor Bases and Enhancers A variety of products—broth, tomatoes, soups, mustard, soy sauce, and prepared fresh herbs—provide moisture and seasonings to infuse what you're slow cooking with terrific taste.

Simple Sides

No-Fuss Rice and Noodles: When the main dish bubbling away in the slow cooker only requires some rice or noodles to make it a meal, call on these preseasoned dry rice and pasta sides. They come in a flavor profile to fit any dish and require only water, a little oil, and a few minutes on the stovetop or microwave to cook.

Fresh in a Flash: There is no easier way to prepare a fresh-vegetable side than with the frozen vegetables that come in a microwavable pouch. Pop it in the microwave, then pour into a serving bowl. Toss corn with fresh basil, green beans with walnuts, and peas with lemon zest and butter.

Rice Is Nice: Hot cooked rice is a fitting accompaniment to many slow cooker dishes—perfect for soaking up those yummy meat juices and creamy sauces. Cook it up plain or pump up the flavor with the addition of some savvy stir-ins. I like to replace some of the water with white wine and/or chicken broth—then sprinkle with some freshly grated Parmesan cheese right before serving.

Baking in a Slow Cooker

Beautiful Brownies: Prepare the brownie mix according to package directions, then follow the slow cooker baking method in Steps 1, 4, 5, and 6 for Gooey Caramel Brownies on page 86. When the brownies are cool, cut and top with raspberry jam and/or Pillsbury® Easy Frost—a fabulous new frosting in a can that comes in vanilla, cream cheese, and chocolate fudge flavors. The built-in star decorating tip allows you to make beautiful swirls effortlessly.

Try a New Topping: Next time you make your favorite slow cooker fruit crisp or cobbler, swap the topping for this sweet idea: Prepare a sugar cookie mix according to package directions, then crumble it over the top of the fruit before baking.

Tip: When you bake in a slow cooker, the condensation that naturally forms on the inside lid of the cooker can drip onto your baked goods and make them soggy. Layer 3 to 6 paper towels under the lid to catch the drips as your cake, brownies, or cobbler bakes.

Heirloom Easy Essentials With a slow cooker and a pantry full of great ingredients and innovative products, your treats will taste just like Grandma's—even if they emerge from the slow cooker instead of the oven.

Wise Wines and Tasty Toasts

Stellar Cellar: A good bottle of wine doesn't have to set you back so much that you can't enjoy it. The wines shown here are all quality, value-priced wines. Most of them cost less than $12 per bottle.

Mulled Merlot: Warm up inside and out with red wine steeped with mulling spices in the slow cooker. Garnish with a cinnamon stick.

Two-Way Toast: Perfect for children or those who prefer nonalcoholic drinks, a flute of chilled sparkling white grape juice garnished with fresh cranberries is festive and fun. To make mulled hot sparkling cider, combine sparkling white grape juice, apple juice, and assorted spices such as cloves, cinnamon sticks, and ribbons of orange peel in a slow cooker. Cook on High for 1 hour or Low for 2 to 3 hours. With a slotted spoon, strain out spices. Ladle into mugs and garnish with fresh cranberries and a cinnamon stick.

Tip: When making mulled cider or wine, you can put the spices in a 6x6-inch double layer of 100-percent cotton cheesecloth tied with kitchen string, or you can just toss them right in the slow cooker. Remove them with a slotted spoon or small mesh strainer before serving.

Entertaining and Gatherings Everyone loves a savory pastry to nibble with a glass of wine—but not many of us have time to play pastry chef at home. Pick up frozen or ready-to-go pastries at the supermarket.

Slow Cooker Sizes and Styles

Get with the Program: Some slow cookers are programmable, which means that before you walk out the door, you set both the cooking time and the temperature too. When it reaches the desired temperature to cooking time, the pot automatically switches to a "warm" setting, so if you are later getting home than you anticipated, your dinner will be perfectly cooked, warm and ready to eat rather than overdone and dried out.

Small Cookers: For single people or couples, a $1^1/_2$-quart cooker is a good option. For couples who like leftovers and for small families, a $3^1/_2$- to $4^1/_2$-quart cooker is the best choice. It's also the right size for soups, stews, and chilies.

Large Cookers: Most of the recipes in this book call for large 4- to 5-quart cookers. This is a good universal size because large families will get their fill and small families will have leftovers to eat the next night or freeze. For very large families, 6- to 8-quart cookers are available. Some large cookers come with a 2-cup cooker that is perfect for keeping sauces and party dips warm for 3 to 4 hours.

Smart Slow Cooking: As simple as it is, it pays to heed a few hints for successful slow cooking. Slow cookers work best when filled between one-half and two-thirds full, so be sure to use the correct size called for in a recipe. Layer the ingredients as directed. Thaw meat—never use frozen—before putting it in the slow cooker. If you have time, you can brown it first, but that's not necessary. And finally, resist the urge to peek. Every time you lift the lid, an additional 15 minutes is added to your cooking time.

Choose a Slow Cooker
With a variety of sizes, shapes, colors, and styles available—made simple and straightforward or with a variety of added features—there is a slow cooker (or two) to suit every family's needs.

Everyday Finger Foods

There's something about the casualness of eating with your hands that puts everyone at ease and in the mood for fun. Whether you're whipping up some yummy nibbles for a simple weeknight gathering or hosting a big Saturday night soirée, the slow cooker makes party prep easy on you. The aroma of Masala Wings or Sesame Teriyaki Ribs bubbling away makes everyone want to linger just a little bit longer.

Adobo Wings

Prep 20 minutes   **Cook** 2 to 3 hours (High)   **Makes** 12 servings

Canola oil cooking spray
2½ pounds chicken wings
2 tablespoons Mexican seasoning
1 teaspoon kosher salt
2 cups chicken broth
1 jar (8.25-ounce) adobo sauce
3 tablespoons maple syrup
2 tablespoons white vinegar
2 teaspoons chopped garlic
2 teaspoons hot pepper sauce
Salt and ground black pepper
Chopped fresh cilantro (optional)

1. Coat a 5-quart slow cooker with cooking spray; set aside.

2. Preheat broiler. Line a baking sheet with aluminum foil; set aside.

3. Sprinkle chicken wings with Mexican seasoning and kosher salt. Place wings on prepared baking sheet. Broil 4 to 6 inches from heat for 8 to 10 minutes or until skin is tender and begins to crisp, turning once.

4. In a medium saucepan, stir together chicken broth, adobo sauce, maple syrup, vinegar, garlic, and hot pepper sauce. Heat thoroughly over medium heat. Season to taste with salt and pepper. Pour some of the sauce in the bottom of slow cooker. Coat wings, a few at a time, with remaining sauce and place in slow cooker. Pour remaining sauce over wings.

5. Cover and cook on High heat setting for 2 to 3 hours.

6. Transfer wings to a serving platter. Spoon sauce over wings. Sprinkle with chopped cilantro (optional).

Masala Wings

Prep 25 minutes   **Cook** 2 hours (Low) + 1½ to 2½ hours (High)   **Makes** 12 servings

Canola oil cooking spray

1	can (10-ounce) diced tomatoes and green chiles
1	can (8-ounce) tomato sauce
1	cup coconut milk
1	small jalapeño, seeded and finely chopped
3	teaspoons garam masala
2	teaspoons chopped garlic
2	teaspoons ginger spice blend
¼	cup butter
¼	teaspoon kosher salt
2½	pounds chicken wings, tips removed
⅓	cup plain yogurt
¾	cup cashews, chopped

1. Coat a 5-quart slow cooker with cooking spray; set aside.

2. In a large bowl, stir together tomatoes, tomato sauce, coconut milk, jalapeño, 2 teaspoons of the garam masala, the garlic, and ginger until combined. Pour into slow cooker. Add butter.

3. Cover and cook on Low heat setting for 2 hours.

4. Fifteen minutes before sauce is done, preheat broiler. Line a baking sheet with aluminum foil; set aside. In a small bowl, combine the remaining 1 teaspoon garam masala and the salt. Sprinkle wings with spice mixture. Place chicken wings on prepared baking sheet. Broil 4 to 6 inches from heat for 10 to 12 minutes or until skin is tender and begins to crisp, turning once.

5. Stir sauce in slow cooker and add wings. Stir gently to coat wings with sauce. Cover and cook on High heat setting for 1½ to 2½ hours.

6. Transfer wings to a serving platter. Skim off any fat from the top of the sauce; stir in yogurt until smooth. Spoon sauce over wings; sprinkle with chopped cashews. Serve immediately.

Barbecued Ranch Ribs

Prep 25 minutes   **Cook** 6 to 8 hours (Low)   **Makes** 6 servings

2   packets (1 ounce each) ranch dressing mix
2   tablespoons paprika
1   tablespoon garlic salt
1   tablespoon salt-free lemon pepper
2   racks pork baby back ribs, cut into single-rib portions
1   bottle (18-ounce) barbecue sauce
1   tablespoon molasses
½   teaspoon hot pepper sauce

1. Preheat broiler. Line a baking sheet with aluminum foil; set aside.

2. In a small bowl, stir together 1 packet of the ranch dressing mix, paprika, garlic salt, and lemon pepper. Rub ribs with mixture. Place ribs on baking sheet, bone sides down. Broil 4 to 6 inches from heat for 10 minutes; turn and broil for 10 minutes more.

3. In a medium bowl, combine remaining ranch dressing mix, barbecue sauce, molasses, and hot pepper sauce. Coat ribs, several at a time, with sauce. Place in a 5-quart slow cooker. Pour remaining sauce over ribs.

4. Cover and cook on Low heat setting for 6 to 8 hours. Transfer ribs to a serving platter.

5. Skim fat from the top of the sauce. Serve sauce on side.

Cheesy Enchilada Meatballs

Prep 15 minutes   **Cook** 4 to 6 hours (Low)   **Makes** 12 servings

1   can (28-ounce) enchilada sauce
1   can (10.75-ounce) condensed cheddar cheese soup, *Campbell's*®
½   teaspoon chipotle chile powder
2   pounds fully cooked frozen meatballs
1½   cups shredded Mexican cheese blend
     Additional shredded Mexican cheese blend (optional)

1. In a large bowl, whisk together enchilada sauce, cheese soup, and chile powder. Pour one-fourth of the sauce into a 5-quart slow cooker. Coat meatballs, several at a time, with remaining sauce and place in slow cooker. Pour remaining sauce over meatballs. Sprinkle 1½ cups shredded cheese over meatballs.

2. Cover and cook on Low heat setting for 4 to 6 hours.

3. Transfer meatballs to a serving dish. Using a wire mesh strainer, strain sauce. Skim off any fat from the top of sauce. Spoon sauce over meatballs. Sprinkle with additional shredded cheese (optional).

Sesame Teriyaki Ribs

Prep 25 minutes   **Cook** 6 to 8 hours (Low)   **Makes** 12 servings

2   racks pork baby back ribs, cut into single-rib portions

1   packet (1.25-ounce) honey teriyaki seasoning mix

1   cup teriyaki marinade and sauce

1   cup pineapple dessert topping

¼   cup cold water

1   tablespoon cornstarch

¼   cup sesame seeds, plus additional toasted* (optional)

Canola oil cooking spray

1. Preheat broiler. Line a baking sheet with aluminum foil; set aside.

2. Rub ribs with seasoning mix. Place ribs, bone sides down, on prepared baking sheet. Broil 4 to 6 inches from heat for 10 minutes; turn and broil for 10 minutes more. Set aside.

3. In a medium bowl, whisk together teriyaki marinade and pineapple dessert topping. In a small bowl, stir together cold water and cornstarch until cornstarch is dissolved; whisk into teriyaki mixture. Stir in ¼ cup sesame seeds. Coat a 5-quart slow cooker with cooking spray. Place ribs, bone sides down, in slow cooker. Pour sauce over ribs.

4. Cover and cook on Low heat setting for 6 to 8 hours. Sprinkle with toasted sesame seeds (optional). Serve with sauce.

***Note:** To toast sesame seeds, spread seeds in a dry large nonstick skillet. Heat over medium-high heat, stirring occasionally, until seeds are golden.

Red Hot Curry Ribs

Prep 10 minutes   **Cook** 6 to 7 hours (Low)   **Makes** 6 servings

1   container (6-ounce) sliced peppers and onions, chopped

1   cup petite-cut diced tomatoes, drained

12   beef short ribs

1   cup coconut milk

½   cup reduced-sodium chicken broth

¼   cup packed brown sugar

3   tablespoons red curry paste

1   tablespoon chopped garlic

2   teaspoons ginger spice blend

Chopped fresh cilantro (optional)

1. In a 5-quart slow cooker, stir together peppers, onions, and tomatoes. Place ribs, bone sides down, in slow cooker. In a medium bowl, whisk together coconut milk, chicken broth, brown sugar, curry paste, garlic, and ginger until combined. Pour over ribs in slow cooker.

2. Cover and cook on Low heat setting for 6 to 7 hours.

3. Using a slotted spoon, transfer ribs and vegetables to a serving platter. Using a wire mesh strainer, strain sauce. Skim off any fat from the top of the sauce. Spoon some sauce over ribs. Sprinkle with cilantro (optional).

Meatballs and Sausages in Cranberry Mustard

Prep 15 minutes   **Cook** 2 to 3 hours (High)   **Makes** 16 servings

1	package (12-ounce) fully cooked garlic and artichoke sausages
1	pound fully cooked frozen meatballs
1	can (16-ounce) whole cranberry sauce
1½	cups chicken broth
½	cup honey-mustard salad dressing
¼	cup Dijon mustard
¾	teaspoon crushed red pepper

1. Cut each sausage into 6 pieces. Place sausages and meatballs in a 5-quart slow cooker. In a medium bowl, whisk together cranberry sauce, chicken broth, salad dressing, mustard, and crushed red pepper. Pour over meatballs and sausages; stir to coat.

2. Cook on High heat setting for 2 to 3 hours.

3. Transfer meatballs and sausages to a serving dish. Using a wire mesh strainer, strain sauce. Skim off any fat from the top of sauce. Spoon sauce over meatballs and sausages.

Hawaiian Drummettes

Prep 20 minutes   **Cook** 2½ to 3½ hours (High)   **Makes** 12 servings

2½	pounds chicken drummettes
2	teaspoons garlic salt
½	cup papaya nectar
½	cup coconut milk
½	cup ginger preserves
3	tablespoons tomato paste
2	teaspoons chopped garlic
1	can (8-ounce) crushed pineapple
⅓	cup frozen chopped green peppers
½	teaspoon crushed red pepper

1. Preheat broiler. Line a baking sheet with aluminum foil; set aside. Sprinkle drummettes with garlic salt. Place drummettes on prepared baking sheet. Broil 4 to 6 inches from heat for 8 to 10 minutes or until skin is tender and begins to crisp, turning once.

2. In a large bowl, whisk together papaya nectar, coconut milk, ginger preserves, tomato paste, and garlic. Stir in pineapple, green peppers, and crushed red pepper until well combined. Coat drummettes, several at a time, with sauce. Place in a 4- or 5-quart slow cooker. Pour remaining sauce over drummettes.

3. Cover and cook on High heat setting for 2½ to 3½ hours.

4. Transfer drummettes to a serving platter. Skim off any fat from the top of sauce. Serve sauce on side.

Spicy Hoisin Drummies

Prep 20 minutes   **Cook** 2½ to 3½ hours (High)   **Makes** 12 servings

1 packet (1.6-ounce) buffalo wings seasoning mix
1 tablespoon garlic salt
2½ pounds chicken drummettes
1 cup hoisin sauce
¼ cup ketchup
3 tablespoons packed dark brown sugar

1. Preheat broiler. Line a baking sheet with aluminum foil; set aside.

2. In a large bowl, stir together seasoning mix and garlic salt. Add drummettes; toss until coated. Place drummettes on prepared baking sheet. Broil 4 to 6 inches from heat for 8 to 10 minutes or until skin is tender and begins to crisp, turning once.

3. In the same large bowl, whisk together hoisin sauce, ketchup, and brown sugar. Coat drummettes, several at a time, with sauce and place in a 4- or 5-quart slow cooker. Pour remaining sauce over drummettes.

4. Cover and cook on High heat setting for 2½ to 3½ hours.

5. Transfer drummettes to a serving platter. Skim off any fat from the top of the cooking liquid; serve on side.

Spicy Cheese and Bacon Dip

Prep 10 minutes   **Cook** 3 to 4 hours (Low)   **Makes** 4 cups

Canola oil cooking spray
1 box (16-ounce) processed cheese, cubed
½ pound pepper Jack cheese, shredded
1 package (8-ounce) cream cheese, softened
1 can (10-ounce) diced tomatoes with habaneros
¾ cup crumbled cooked bacon
¼ cup diced green chiles
½ teaspoon hot pepper sauce
Tortilla chips

1. Coat a 4-quart slow cooker with cooking spray. In slow cooker, stir together cheeses, tomatoes, bacon, chiles, and hot pepper sauce.

2. Cover and cook on Low heat setting for 3 to 4 hours, stirring once halfway through cooking time. Serve dip warm with tortilla chips.

Hot Reuben Dip

Prep 10 minutes   **Cook** 1 to 2 hours (Low)   **Makes** 12 servings

1¾ cups sauerkraut, drained

1½ cups shredded Swiss cheese

1 package (8-ounce) cream cheese, softened

1 cup shredded Gruyère cheese

½ pound deli corned beef, chopped

⅓ cup Thousand Island salad dressing

¼ cup frozen chopped onions

Rye crackers

1. In a 4-quart slow cooker, combine sauerkraut, cheeses, corned beef, salad dressing, and onions.

2. Cover and cook on Low heat setting for 1 to 2 hours, stirring occasionally. Serve dip warm with rye crackers.

Spinach-Artichoke Dip

Prep 10 minutes   **Cook** 2½ to 3½ hours (Low)   **Makes** 6 cups

Canola oil cooking spray

2 boxes (10 ounces each) frozen spinach, thawed and squeezed dry

1 can (13.75-ounce) quartered artichoke hearts, drained and chopped

1 can (10.5-ounce) white sauce

1½ cups shredded mozzarella cheese

1 package (8-ounce) cream cheese, cut into cubes

½ cup frozen chopped onions

¼ cup shredded Parmesan cheese

2 teaspoons chopped garlic

½ cup sour cream

Salt and ground black pepper

Blue corn tortilla chips

1. Coat a 4-quart slow cooker with cooking spray. In the slow cooker, stir together spinach, artichoke hearts, white sauce, mozzarella cheese, cream cheese, onions, Parmesan cheese, and garlic until combined.

2. Cover and cook on Low heat setting for 2½ to 3½ hours, stirring once halfway through cooking time. During the last ½ hour of cooking, stir in sour cream. Season to taste with salt and pepper. Serve dip warm with tortilla chips.

Meals in a Bowl

There are few foods more comforting than soup—especially when I can put it on in the morning and forget about it until late-afternoon hunger pangs remind me that I don't have to worry about what to make for dinner. When I walk through the door after a long day to the delicious aroma of homemade soup, I immediately begin to unwind.

Greek Beef Stew

Prep 10 minutes   **Cook** 4 to 6 hours (High)   **Makes** 4 servings

1   container (17-ounce) beef tips in gravy

1   can (14.5-ounce) diced tomatoes with garlic, oregano, and basil

1   bag (14-ounce) frozen petite whole onions

1   can (14-ounce) reduced-sodium beef broth

1   package (8-ounce) sliced mushrooms

⅓   cup red wine

1   envelope (1-ounce) onion soup mix

1   tablespoon red wine vinegar

2   teaspoons Mediterranean salad seasoning

2   teaspoons ground cinnamon

2   teaspoons chopped garlic

     Salt and ground black pepper

1. In a 4-quart slow cooker, stir together beef tips, tomatoes, onions, beef broth, mushrooms, wine, onion soup mix, vinegar, salad seasoning, cinnamon, and garlic until combined.

2. Cover and cook on High heat setting for 4 to 6 hours. Season to taste with salt and pepper.

Cowboy Stew

Prep 10 minutes   **Cook** 4 to 6 hours (High)   **Makes** 6 servings

1   2-pound beef brisket, trimmed and cut into bite-size pieces

1   packet (1.25-ounce) hot taco seasoning mix

2   cups finely chopped red potatoes

1   can (16-ounce) diced tomatoes and green chiles

1   can (10.75-ounce) condensed cream of celery soup, *Campbell's*®

1   cup frozen corn kernels

1   cup reduced-sodium beef broth

¾   cup frozen chopped onions

2   teaspoons chopped garlic

1. Sprinkle brisket pieces with taco seasoning mix. In a 4-quart slow cooker, stir together brisket pieces, potatoes, tomatoes, celery soup, corn, beef broth, onions, and garlic until combined.

2. Cover and cook on High heat setting for 4 to 6 hours.

Ham-Split Pea Soup

Prep 10 minutes   **Cook** 6 to 8 hours (Low)   **Makes** 8 servings

4	cups water
3	cups beef broth
1	pound dry split peas
2	cups cubed ham
1½	cups frozen chopped onions
1	cup frozen sliced carrots
4	celery sticks, finely chopped
2	teaspoons dried thyme
	Salt and ground black pepper
	Seasoned croutons (optional)

1. In a 5-quart slow cooker, stir together water, beef broth, split peas, ham, onions, carrots, celery, and thyme until combined.

2. Cover and cook on Low heat setting for 6 to 8 hours.

3. Season to taste with salt and pepper. Spoon into soup bowls. Sprinkle croutons on top (optional).

Brazilian Spare Rib Stew

Prep 20 minutes   **Cook** 4 to 5 hours (High)   **Makes** 10 servings

⅓	cup finely chopped salt pork*
4	cans (15 ounces each) black beans, rinsed and drained
4	cups reduced-sodium beef broth
1	pound pork spare ribs, cut into single-rib portions
1	package (13-ounce) linguica sausage links, sliced
1	bag (4-ounce) beef jerky
1	cup frozen chopped onions
1	cup water
1	tablespoon chopped garlic
1	teaspoon red pepper flakes
1	bay leaf
	Chopped fresh flat-leaf parsley (optional)
	Hot pepper sauce (optional)

1. In a medium skillet, over medium-high heat, cook salt pork for 6 to 8 minutes or until browned.

2. In a 5-quart slow cooker, stir together browned salt pork, beans, beef broth, ribs, sausage, beef jerky, onions, water, garlic, red pepper flakes, and bay leaf until combined.

3. Cover and cook on High heat setting for 4 to 5 hours.

4. Remove and discard bay leaf. Spoon stew into soup bowls. Sprinkle with parsley and serve with hot sauce (optional).

*Note: Substitute 6 slices of bacon, chopped, for salt pork.

Tuscan Peasant Soup

Prep 15 minutes   **Cook** 3 to 4 hours (High)   **Makes** 6 servings

1   package (16-ounce) hot Italian sausage links, *Johnsonville*®

4   cups reduced-sodium beef broth

1   can (15-ounce) cannellini beans, rinsed and drained

1   can (14.5-ounce) diced tomatoes with Italian herbs

1   bag (14-ounce) frozen Tuscan vegetable blend

1   can (8-ounce) tomato sauce

2   teaspoons dried Italian seasoning

2   teaspoons chopped garlic

    Salt and ground black pepper

1   cup shredded Parmesan cheese

    Prepared frozen garlic bread (optional)

1. In a large skillet, over medium-high heat, brown sausages on all sides. Remove from skillet; let cool to the touch. Cut into bite-size pieces.

2. In a 4-quart slow cooker, stir together sausage, beef broth, beans, tomatoes, vegetable blend, tomato sauce, Italian seasoning, and garlic until combined.

3. Cover and cook on High heat setting for 3 to 4 hours.

4. Season to taste with salt and pepper. Spoon into soup bowls. Sprinkle with Parmesan cheese. Serve soup with garlic bread (optional).

Cancun Chicken Soup

Prep 10 minutes   **Cook** 3 to 4 hours (High)   **Makes** 6 servings

2   cans (15 ounces each) white hominy, rinsed and drained

3½   cups reduced-sodium chicken broth

1   pound chicken tenders, cut into bite-size pieces

1   cup frozen chopped onions

½   cup sliced jalapeños

1   can (4-ounce) diced mild green chiles

1   tablespoon chopped garlic

2   teaspoons poultry seasoning

    Salt and ground black pepper

3   tablespoons chopped cilantro (optional)

    Hot pepper sauce (optional)

    Lime wedges (optional)

1. In a 4-quart slow cooker, stir together hominy, chicken broth, chicken, onions, jalapeños, chiles, garlic, and poultry seasoning until combined.

2. Cover and cook on High heat setting for 3 to 4 hours.

3. Season to taste with salt and pepper. Spoon into soup bowls. Sprinkle with cilantro (optional). Serve with hot sauce and lime wedges (optional).

Chile Chicken Chowder

Prep 10 minutes   **Cook** 3 to 4 hours (High)   **Makes** 6 servings

1¼   pounds chicken tenders, cut into bite-size pieces

1½   cups diced potatoes

1½   cups reduced-sodium chicken broth

1   can (14.75-ounce) cream-style corn

1   can (10.75-ounce) condensed cream of chicken soup, *Campbell's*®

1   can (7-ounce) diced mild green chiles

½   cup frozen chopped onions

2   teaspoons chopped garlic

1   teaspoon ground cumin

½   cup half-and-half

      Chopped fresh cilantro (optional)

1. In a 4-quart slow cooker, stir together chicken, potatoes, chicken broth, corn, chicken soup, chile peppers, onions, garlic, and cumin until combined.

2. Cover and cook on High heat setting for 3 to 4 hours.

3. Stir in half-and-half. Spoon into soup bowls. Sprinkle with cilantro (optional).

Curried Chicken Apple Stew

Prep 10 minutes   **Cook** 3 to 4 hours (High)   **Makes** 6 servings

4½   cups chicken broth

2   cups chopped boneless, skinless chicken breast

2   cups chopped red and green apple slices

1½   cups coconut milk

1   cup frozen chopped onions

2   teaspoons ginger spice blend

½   teaspoon curry powder

½   teaspoon ground cumin

1   package (8.8-ounce) ready rice

      Salt and ground black pepper

1   tablespoon lemon juice

½   cup sliced almonds

1. In a 5-quart slow cooker, stir together chicken broth, chicken, apples, coconut milk, onions, ginger, curry powder, and cumin until combined.

2. Cover and cook on High heat setting for 3 to 4 hours. During the last ½ hour of cooking time, stir in rice.

3. Season to taste with salt and pepper. Just before serving, stir in lemon juice and sliced almonds.

Creamy Turkey Stew

Prep 10 minutes   **Cook** 4 to 6 hours (High)   **Makes** 6 servings

1¼ pounds turkey breast cutlets, cut into strips

2 packages (8 ounces each) sliced fresh mushrooms

2 cups diced potatoes

1½ cups finely chopped carrot and celery sticks

1 cup frozen white corn kernels

2 cups reduced-sodium chicken broth

1 can (10.75-ounce) condensed cream of potato soup, *Campbell's*®

1 packet (0.87-ounce) chicken gravy mix

½ teaspoon dried tarragon

Salt and ground black pepper

Crumbled cooked bacon (optional)

Chopped fresh flat-leaf parsley (optional)

1. In a 5-quart slow cooker, stir together turkey, mushrooms, potatoes, carrots and celery, and corn until combined. In a large bowl, whisk together chicken broth, potato soup, gravy mix, and tarragon. Pour into slow cooker; stir until combined.

2. Cover and cook on High heat setting for 4 to 6 hours.

3. Season to taste with salt and pepper. Spoon into soup bowls. Sprinkle with crumbled bacon and parsley (optional).

Coconut Seafood Stew

Prep 30 minutes   **Cook** 6 to 8 hours (Low) + 30 minutes (High)   **Makes** 4 servings

1   can (14.5-ounce) light coconut milk

1   can (15-ounce) baby corn, drained

8   ounces bottled clam juice

4   medium red potatoes, quartered and parboiled

2   serrano chiles, thinly sliced (optional)

1   cup dry white wine

1   jar (4-ounce) green curry sauce

½   cup fresh sweet basil leaves

1   tablespoon chopped garlic

½   teaspoon freshly ground black pepper

1   pound shrimp (16 to 21 count), peeled

4   cooked king crab legs, split, each approximately 6 inches long

12   steamer clams

8   large mussels, scrubbed and beards removed

    Kosher salt

1. In a 5-quart slow cooker, stir together coconut milk, corn, clam juice, potatoes, serrano chiles (optional), wine, curry sauce, basil, garlic, and black pepper.

2. Cover and cook on Low heat setting for 6 to 8 hours.

3. Turn slow cooker to High heat setting. Stir in shrimp, crab legs, clams, and mussels. Cover and cook for 30 minutes more or until shrimp is opaque and clams and mussels have opened. Remove and discard any clams or mussels that have not opened. Season to taste with salt.

French Garden Chowder

Prep 15 minutes   **Cook** 3 to 4 hours (High)   **Makes** 6 servings

2   cans (10.75 ounces each) condensed cream of potato soup, *Campbell's*®

2½   cups vegetable broth

1   can (14.5-ounce) diced tomatoes, drained

1   can (13.75-ounce) quartered artichoke hearts, drained

1   box (10-ounce) frozen asparagus cuts

1   bag (8-ounce) haricots verts, halved

1   medium leek, halved lengthwise, cleaned, and sliced

2   teaspoons chopped garlic

2   teaspoons herbes de Provence

½   cup half-and-half

      Salt and ground black pepper

      Crusty French baguette (optional)

1. In a 4-quart slow cooker, stir together potato soup, vegetable broth, tomatoes, artichoke hearts, asparagus, haricots verts, leek, garlic, and herbes de Provence until combined.

2. Cover and cook on High heat setting for 3 to 4 hours.

3. Stir in half-and-half. Season to taste with salt and pepper. Serve chowder with baguette slices (optional).

Hearty Vegetable Soup

Prep 15 minutes   **Cook** 4 to 5 hours (High)   **Makes** 8 servings

2   cans (15.25 ounces each) kidney beans

2   cans (15 ounces each) white beans (navy or Great Northern)

1   can (28-ounce) crushed tomatoes

3   cups vegetable broth

1   can (15-ounce) black beans

2   cups shredded cabbage

1½   cups frozen sliced carrots

1   cup chopped onions

½   cup pearl barley

4   celery sticks, chopped

2   tablespoons red wine vinegar

1   packet (1.25-ounce) hunter sauce mix

1   bay leaf

     Salt and ground black pepper

1. In a 5-quart slow cooker, stir together kidney beans, white beans, tomatoes, vegetable broth, black beans, cabbage, carrots, onions, barley, celery, vinegar, hunter sauce mix, and bay leaf until combined.

2. Cover and cook on High heat setting for 4 to 5 hours.

3. Remove and discard bay leaf. Season soup to taste with salt and pepper.

Gatherings and Get-Togethers

Having friends and family over for good food and celebration is one of the greatest joys of my life. And like all busy cooks, I can always use the help the slow cooker provides in putting on a party. Whether you're hosting the holidays or another kind of gathering, these recipes for drinks, appetizers, main dishes, side dishes, and desserts (including a slow-cooked Pumpkin Spice Cheesecake!) allow you to have fun too.

Cran-Apple Cinnamon Toddy

Prep 10 minutes   **Cook** 1 to 2 hours (Low)   **Makes** 4 servings

2   cups apple cider

1   cup cranberry juice cocktail

½   cup spiced rum

¼   cup cinnamon schnapps

4   sticks cinnamon (plus more for garnish [optional])

1. In a 4-quart slow cooker, stir together apple cider, cranberry juice cocktail, rum, schnapps, and cinnamon.

2. Cover and cook on Low heat setting for 1 to 2 hours. Remove and discard cinnamon sticks.

3. Serve hot toddy warm in clear, footed coffee mugs with fresh cinnamon stick swizzles (optional).

Sweet and Spicy Pecans

Prep 10 minutes   **Cook** 3 hours (Low) + 30 minutes (High)   **Makes** 4 cups

3   tablespoons packed dark brown sugar

1   teaspoon pumpkin pie spice

½   teaspoon kosher salt

¼   teaspoon ground black pepper

½   teaspoon cayenne pepper

Canola oil cooking spray

4   cups pecans halves

⅓   cup butter, melted

Chopped fresh flat-leaf parsley (optional)

1. In a small bowl, stir together brown sugar, pumpkin pie spice, salt, black pepper, and cayenne pepper until combined.

2. Coat a 4-quart slow cooker with cooking spray. Place pecans in slow cooker. Pour melted butter over pecans and toss to coat. Sprinkle spice mixture over pecans; toss until well coated.

3. Cover and cook on Low heat setting for 3 hours, stirring once every hour. Turn slow cooker to High heat setting. Remove lid and cook for 30 minutes more.

4. Serve immediately or turn slow cooker to Warm heat setting; keep warm. Sprinkle with parsley (optional).

Cranberry-Orange Baked Brie

Prep 20 minutes   **Cook** 2 to 2½ hours (High)   **Bake** 25 minutes   **Makes** 12 servings

Canola oil cooking spray

1 bag (12-ounce) fresh or frozen cranberries

¾ cup sugar

½ cup orange juice

½ cup orange marmalade

1 stick cinnamon

1 sheet frozen puff pastry, thawed

1 wheel (13.2-ounce) Brie

1 egg, lightly beaten with 1 teaspoon water

Assorted crackers

1. Coat a 4-quart slow cooker with cooking spray. In slow cooker, stir together cranberries, sugar, orange juice, and marmalade until combined. Add cinnamon stick.

2. Cover and cook on High heat setting for 2 to 2½ hours, stirring at least once.

3. Remove and discard cinnamon stick. Remove cover from slow cooker; let sauce cool.

4. Meanwhile, preheat oven to 400 degrees F. Spray a baking sheet with cooking spray; set aside. Unroll puff pastry sheet and lay flat. Place Brie wheel in the center of puff pastry. Bring ends of puff pastry over cheese toward the center of wheel. Securely fold ends under; lay wrapped wheel, fold side down, on prepared baking sheet. Brush pastry with egg wash. Bake in preheated oven for 25 minutes. Let cool for 10 minutes before serving.

5. Place baked Brie on serving platter. Spoon cranberry-orange sauce over top. Serve warm with assorted crackers.

Peppermint Hot Chocolate

Prep 10 minutes   **Cook** 2 to 3 hours (Low)   **Makes** 8 servings

6 cans (12 ounces each) evaporated milk

⅓ cup chocolate liqueur

¼ cup peppermint schnapps

2 bags (12 ounces each) dark chocolate chips

Whipped dessert topping (optional)

Candy canes (optional)

1. In a 4-quart slow cooker, whisk together evaporated milk, chocolate liqueur, and peppermint schnapps. Add chocolate chips.

2. Cover and cook on Low heat setting for 2 to 3 hours, stirring every 15 to 20 minutes.

3. Top each mug of hot chocolate with a spoonful of whipped topping (optional) and place a candy cane (optional) on the lip of the mug.

Sunday Supper Roast Beef

Prep 20 minutes   **Cook** 8 to 10 hours (Low)   **Makes** 6 servings

1   pound baby Yukon gold potatoes

2   cups frozen carrots

1   large onion, chopped

1   stalk celery, chopped

1   tablespoon garlic-herb seasoning blend

1   3-pound beef rump roast

1   packet (1-ounce) onion soup mix

1   jar (12-ounce) mushroom gravy

1   tablespoon chopped garlic

1. In a 5-quart slow cooker, toss together potatoes, carrots, onion, celery, and garlic-herb seasoning. Sprinkle both sides of roast with onion soup mix. Place on top of vegetables in slow cooker.

2. In a small bowl, stir together gravy and garlic. Pour over roast in slow cooker.

3. Cover and cook on Low heat setting for 8 to 10 hours.

4. Transfer roast to a cutting board; let rest for 10 minutes before slicing. Serve sliced roast with vegetables and gravy.

Pork Roast and Cranberry Dressing

Prep 15 minutes   **Cook** 5 to 6 hours (Low)   **Stand** 15 minutes   **Makes** 6 servings

1½   cups frozen chopped onions

2   stalks celery, chopped

1   3-pound boneless pork shoulder roast

2   tablespoons Montreal steak seasoning

1   can (16-ounce) whole cranberry sauce

½   cup dry white wine

1   cup vegetable broth

¼   cup butter

1   box (6-ounce) pork stuffing mix

¾   cup sweetened dried cranberries

1. In a 5-quart slow cooker, combine onions and celery. Sprinkle roast with steak seasoning; place on vegetables in slow cooker. In a medium bowl, stir together cranberry sauce and wine until combined. Spoon over roast in slow cooker.

2. Cover and cook on Low heat setting for 5 to 6 hours.

3. Transfer roast to a cutting board; let rest for 10 minutes before slicing.

4. Meanwhile, in a medium saucepan, over high heat, bring vegetable broth and butter to a boil. Stir pork stuffing mix and dried cranberries into pan. Cover and remove from heat. Let sit for 5 minutes, then fluff with a fork.

5. To serve, mound some stuffing on center of plate. Spoon a portion of celery, onions, cranberries, and accumulated juices from slow cooker over stuffing. Top with sliced roast.

Cinnamon-Glazed Ham

Prep 10 minutes   **Cook** 5 to 6 hours (Low)   **Stand** 10 minutes   **Makes** 6 servings

1	bag (16-ounce) baby carrots
2	tablespoons cinnamon sugar
1	3-pound smoked picnic ham
1	cup orange marmalade
¼	cup apple juice
2	teaspoons ground cinnamon

1. In a 5-quart slow cooker, toss together carrots and cinnamon sugar. Place ham on top of carrots. In a medium bowl, stir together marmalade, apple juice, and cinnamon until smooth. Pour over ham in slow cooker.

2. Cover and cook on Low heat setting for 5 to 6 hours.

3. Transfer ham to a cutting board; let rest for 10 minutes before slicing. Serve sliced ham with carrots and glaze.

Mexi-Scalloped Corn

Prep 15 minutes   **Cook** 2 to 2½ hours (High)   **Makes** 8 servings

Canola oil cooking spray

2   cans (11 ounces each) Mexicorn, drained

1   can (14.75-ounce) creamed corn

3   eggs

½   cup evaporated milk

½   cup corn muffin mix

¼   cup butter, melted

3   tablespoons bourbon

Salt and ground black pepper

1. Coat a 4-quart slow cooker with cooking spray. In slow cooker, stir together mexicorn and creamed corn.

2. In a medium bowl, whisk together eggs, evaporated milk, muffin mix, melted butter, and bourbon until combined. Pour over corn in slow cooker; stir until combined. Season to taste with salt and pepper.

3. Cover and cook on High heat setting for 2 to 2½ hours or until set.

Best Green Bean Casserole

Prep 15 minutes   **Cook** 3 to 4 hours (Low)   **Bake** 20 minutes   **Makes** 10 servings

Canola oil cooking spray

2   bags (16 ounces each) frozen cut green beans

2   jars (4.5 ounces each) sliced mushrooms, drained

1   container (6-ounce) french-fried onions

½   cup crumbled cooked bacon

2   teaspoons table-blend seasoning

2   cans (10.75 ounces each) condensed cream of mushroom soup, *Campbell's*®

5   ounces processed cheese, cut into 1-inch cubes

1. Coat a 4-quart slow cooker with cooking spray. In slow cooker, stir together green beans, mushrooms, half of the french-fried onions, the bacon, and seasoning until combined.

2. In a medium bowl, stir together mushroom soup and processed cheese until combined. Pour over vegetables in slow cooker.

3. Cover and cook on Low heat setting for 3 to 4 hours.

4. Thirty minutes before casserole is done, preheat oven to 375 degrees F. On a baking sheet, spread the remaining french-fried onions in a single layer. Bake in preheated oven for 20 minutes. Before serving, sprinkle onions over casserole.

Spicy Candied Sweet Potatoes

Prep 10 minutes **Cook** 2 to 3 hours (Low) + 15 minutes (Low) **Makes** 8 servings

Canola oil cooking spray

2 cans (29 ounces each) cut sweet potatoes, drained

½ cup finely chopped pecans

6 tablespoons butter, cut into small pieces

2 tablespoons frozen orange juice concentrate, thawed

⅓ cup packed brown sugar

2 teaspoons pumpkin pie spice

¼ teaspoon cayenne pepper

3 cups miniature marshmallows

1. Coat a 5-quart slow cooker with cooking spray. In a large bowl, stir together sweet potatoes, pecans, butter, and orange juice concentrate until combined. In a small bowl, stir together brown sugar, pumpkin pie spice, and cayenne pepper until combined. Sprinkle over sweet potato mixture; stir until combined. Spoon into slow cooker.

2. Cover and cook on Low heat setting for 2 to 3 hours.

3. Sprinkle marshmallows over top of sweet potatoes in slow cooker. Cover and cook on Low heat setting for 15 minutes more or until marshmallows are melted.

Grandma Dicie's Stuffing

Prep 10 minutes **Cook** 1 hour (High) + 3 to 4 hours (Low) **Makes** 12 servings

Canola oil cooking spray

3 bags (6 ounces each) seasoned stuffing mix

1 can (15-ounce) reduced-sodium chicken broth

1½ cups frozen chopped onions

1 cup chopped celery

1 cup butter, melted

¾ cup chopped walnuts

½ cup crumbled cooked bacon

1 can (16-ounce) whole cranberry sauce

1. Coat a 5-quart slow cooker with cooking spray; set aside. In a large bowl, toss together stuffing mix, chicken broth, onions, celery, melted butter, walnuts, and bacon until combined. Fold in cranberry sauce. Pour into slow cooker.

2. Cover and cook on High heat setting for 1 hour. Switch to Low heat setting and cook for 3 to 4 hours.

Apple-Pecan Bread Pudding

Prep 15 minutes   **Cook** 3 to 4 hours (Low)   **Makes** 6 servings

Canola oil cooking spray

1 loaf (16-ounce) cinnamon bread, cut into 1-inch cubes

1 can (21-ounce) apple pie filling

1½ cups chopped pecans

1 can (12-ounce) evaporated milk

1½ cups heavy cream

3 eggs

¾ cup packed brown sugar

½ teaspoon ground allspice

Pinch salt

2 tablespoons butter, cut into tiny pieces

¾ cup caramel topping

2 tablespoons bourbon

Whipped dessert topping, thawed (optional)

1. Coat a 5-quart slow cooker with cooking spray. In a large bowl, stir together bread, pie filling, and pecans until combined.

2. In a medium bowl, whisk together evaporated milk, cream, eggs, brown sugar, allspice, and salt until combined. Pour over bread mixture; stir gently until bread is saturated. Pour into slow cooker and dot with butter.

3. Cover and cook on Low heat setting for 3 to 4 hours.

4. In a small microwave-safe bowl, stir together caramel topping and bourbon. Cover and microwave on High setting (100 percent power) for 1 to 2 minutes or until warm. Serve bread pudding topped with caramel-bourbon sauce and whipped topping (optional).

Pumpkin Spice Cheesecake

Prep 30 minutes   **Cook** 1½ to 2 hours (High)   **Stand** 30 minutes   **Chill** 4 hours   **Makes** 8 servings

Canola oil cooking spray

3 cups gingersnaps

2 tablespoons sugar

6 tablespoons butter, melted

2 packages (8 ounces each) plus 2 tablespoons cream cheese, softened

1 cup packed brown sugar

¾ cup pure pumpkin puree

2 teaspoons pumpkin pie spice

3 eggs

6 tablespoons sour cream

1. Coat an 8½-inch springform pan with cooking spray. Wrap foil around the bottom of pan. Crumple additional aluminum foil to create a "ring base" about 5 inches in diameter and 1 inch thick. Set aside.

2. In a food processor, process gingersnaps and sugar into fine crumbs. Add melted butter; pulse until mixture comes together. Press crumbs into bottom of prepared springform pan.

3. In a large bowl, beat cream cheese with an electric mixer on low speed until smooth. Add sugar, pumpkin, and pumpkin pie spice; beat until smooth. Add eggs, one at a time, beating well after each addition. Scrape down sides of bowl. Add sour cream; beat until combined. Pour over crumb crust in springform pan.

4. Place foil ring in bottom of slow cooker; pour ½ inch of hot water into bottom of slow cooker. Using 2 long strips of foil, make an "X" over foil ring and bring it up along the sides of slow cooker to assist removing springform pan from slow cooker. Place springform pan on top of ring and the "X" in slow cooker. Stack 6 paper towels; place over top of slow cooker (to absorb moisture). Secure with lid.

5. Cook on High heat setting for 1½ to 2 hours or until cheesecake is set with a wet-looking center. (Do not lift lid for the first 1 hour of cooking.) Turn off heat and let sit, covered, for 30 minutes.

6. Use foil strips to lift springform pan from slow cooker. Place pan on wire rack; let cool to room temperature. Chill in pan for at least 4 hours. Just before serving, remove cake from pan.

Desserts

My grandma always said that serving a special dessert is a way to show you care. So how do you find time to do what you need to do every day and still savor the sweet things in life? Here's the secret: Use your slow cooker to make these supersimple cakes, cheesecakes, brownies, and fruit desserts. You'll love the delicious results.

Mixed-Berry Buckle

Prep 10 minutes   **Cook** 2 to 3 hours (High)   **Bake** 14 to 16 minutes   **Makes** 8 servings

Canola oil cooking spray

5   cups frozen strawberries

1   can (15-ounce) blackberries in light syrup, drained (reserve ¾ cup syrup)

½   cup raspberry preserves

2   tablespoons instant tapioca

1   box (18.25-ounce) wild blueberry muffin mix

1   cup old-fashioned oats

½   cup butter, melted

Vanilla bean ice cream (optional)

1. Coat a 5-quart slow cooker with cooking spray. In a large bowl, stir together strawberries, blackberries with ¾ cup reserved syrup, the preserves, tapioca, and blueberries from muffin mix until combined. Pour into slow cooker.

2. Cover and cook on High heat setting for 2 to 3 hours.

3. Thirty minutes before serving, preheat oven to 375 degrees F. Line a baking sheet with aluminum foil; set aside. In a medium bowl, use a fork to stir together muffin mix, oats, and melted butter until mixture is coarse with large-size chunks. Spread on prepared baking sheet. Bake in preheated oven for 14 to 16 minutes or until light brown.

4. To serve, sprinkle baked topping over warm mixed berries. Serve with vanilla ice cream (optional).

Hot Cocoa Cherries

Prep 10 minutes   **Cook** 1 hour (low) + 2 to 3 hours (High)   **Makes** 4½ cups

1	cup half-and-half
¾	cup sugar
½	cup butter
6	tablespoons cocoa powder
2	bags (16 ounces each) frozen cherries
¼	cup chocolate liqueur
1	tablespoon cornstarch
2	teaspoons vanilla extract
	Vanilla bean ice cream (optional)
	Chocolate wafer cookies (optional)

1. In a 4-quart slow cooker, stir together half-and-half, sugar, butter, and cocoa powder.

2. Cover and cook on Low heat setting for 1 hour.

3. Remove lid and stir in cherries, liqueur, cornstarch, and vanilla extract. Cook, uncovered, on High heat setting for 2 to 3 hours or until cherries are warm and chocolate mixture is thickened.

4. Serve cherry mixture warm over ice cream with chocolate wafer cookies (optional).

Apricot-Peach Passion Pound Cake

Prep 15 minutes   **Cook** 4 to 5 hours (High)   **Makes** 3 cups

2   cans (8.5 ounces each) apricot halves, drained (reserve juice from 1 can)

1   can (15.25-ounce) sliced peaches, drained

6   tablespoons packed brown sugar

2   teaspoons lemon juice

2   teaspoons apple cider vinegar

1   teaspoon ground cinnamon

1   teaspoon vanilla extract

2   envelopes (0.25 ounce each) unflavored gelatin

    Premade pound cake slices

    Ice cream, for serving (optional)

1. In a blender, blend apricots, reserved apricot juice, and the peaches until smooth; pour into 4-quart slow cooker. Stir in brown sugar, lemon juice, vinegar, cinnamon, and vanilla.

2. Cover and cook on High heat setting for 2 to 2½ hours.

3. Remove lid and stir in gelatin. Cover and cook on High heat setting for 2 to 2½ hours or until desired thickness.

4. Serve fruit mixture warm over sliced pound cake with ice cream (optional). Store in an airtight container in the refrigerator for up to 2 weeks.

Tropical Poached Peaches

Prep 10 minutes   **Cook** 4 to 5 hours (Low)   **Boil** 15 minutes   **Makes** 8 servings

2   bags (16 ounces each) frozen sliced peaches

1   bottle (750 ml) Chardonnay wine

1   cup frozen passion-orange juice concentrate

½   cup packed brown sugar

1   stick cinnamon

2   bags chai spice tea

    Coconut sorbet or vanilla ice cream (optional)

1   cup sweetened shredded coconut, toasted (optional)

1. In a 4-quart slow cooker, stir together peaches, wine, juice concentrate, brown sugar, and cinnamon. Add tea bags.

2. Cover and cook on Low heat setting for 2 hours. Remove and discard tea bags. Cook for 2 to 3 hours more.

3. Pour juice from slow cooker into a medium saucepan. Bring to a boil over medium-high heat. Boil until sauce is reduced and syrupy, about 15 minutes. Remove and discard cinnamon stick. Serve warm peaches and sauce over coconut sorbet (optional). Top with toasted coconut (optional).

Gooey Caramel Brownies

Prep 20 minutes   **Cook** 2½ to 3½ hours (High)   **Makes** 8 servings

Canola oil cooking spray

1 box (18.3-ounce) fudge brownie mix

3 eggs

⅔ cup canola oil

¼ cup, plus 2 tablespoons caramel topping

¼ cup vanilla cream soda

1 cup marshmallow creme

2 tablespoons self-rising flour

1. Coat an 8×3-inch round cake pan with cooking spray. Crumple aluminum foil to create a "ring base" about 5 inches in diameter and 1 inch thick; set aside.

2. In a large bowl, stir together brownie mix, 2 of the eggs, the oil, ¼ cup of the caramel topping, and the cream soda until combined. Pour into prepared pan; set aside.

3. In a large bowl, beat marshmallow creme, flour, the remaining egg, and remaining 2 tablespoons caramel topping with an electric mixer on medium speed until smooth. Pour over brownie batter in pan. Using a knife, make a swirl pattern in creme mixture.

4. Place foil ring in bottom of slow cooker; pour ½ inch of hot water into bottom of slow cooker. Using 2 long strips of foil, make an "X" over foil ring and bring it up along the sides of slow cooker to assist removing pan from slow cooker. Place pan on top of ring and the "X" in slow cooker. Stack 6 paper towels; place over top of slow cooker bowl. Secure with lid.

5. Cook on High heat setting for 2½ to 3½ hours.

6. Use foil strips to lift pan from slow cooker. Place pan on wire rack; cool completely.

Strawberry Cream Cake

Prep 25 minutes   **Cook** 1½ to 2½ hours (High)   **Cool** 60 minutes   **Makes** 8 servings

Canola oil cooking spray

1   box (18.25-ounce) strawberry cake mix

1¼   cups strawberry-banana nectar

3   eggs

½   cup sour cream

⅓   cup canola oil

¼   cup cake flour

2   cans (12 ounces each) whipped cream cheese frosting

1   cup frozen (thawed) or fresh strawberries, sliced (plus more for garnish [optional])

1. Coat an 8×3-inch round cake pan with cooking spray. Wrap foil around the bottom of pan. Crumple additional aluminum foil to create a "ring base" about 5 inches in diameter and 1 inch thick. Set aside.

2. In a large bowl, beat cake mix, nectar, eggs, sour cream, oil, and flour with an electric mixer on low speed for 30 seconds. Scrape down sides of bowl; beat for 2 minutes on medium speed. Pour batter into prepared pan.

3. Place foil ring in bottom of slow cooker; pour ½ inch of hot water into bottom of slow cooker. Using 2 long strips of foil, make an "X" over foil ring and bring it up along the sides of slow cooker to assist removing pan from slow cooker. Place pan on top of ring and the "X" in slow cooker. Stack 6 paper towels; place on top of slow cooker. Secure with lid.

4. Cook on High heat setting for 1½ to 2½ hours* or until a wooden tester inserted into center of cake comes out clean. (Do not lift the lid for the first 1 hour of cooking.)

5. Use foil strips to lift pan from slow cooker. Place pan on wire rack; cool completely.

6. Meanwhile, in a medium bowl, stir together 1 cup of the cream cheese frosting with sliced strawberries until combined. Refrigerate until ready to use.

7. To assemble, remove cooled cake from pan and slice horizontally to make two layers. Place one layer on serving plate. Spread strawberry filling evenly over layer and top with second cake layer. Frost entire cake with remaining cream cheese frosting. Garnish with fresh strawberries.

*Note: If your slow cooker has "hot spots" and a removable liner, rotate liner every hour of cooking.

Gingerbread Pudding Cake

Prep 15 minutes　　**Cook** 2 to 3 hours (Low)　　**Makes** 8 servings

Canola oil cooking spray

1　box (14.5-ounce) gingerbread cake and cookie mix

1　box (15-ounce) honey corn bread muffin mix

2　cups half-and-half

4　eggs

⅔　cup sour cream

6　tablespoons molasses

¼　cup sugar

1　tablespoon ground cinnamon

2　teaspoons ground nutmeg

1　cup golden raisins

Vanilla bean ice cream (optional)

1. Cut parchment paper to fit the bottom of a 5-quart slow cooker. Coat parchment paper and slow cooker with cooking spray. Set aside.

2. In a large bowl, beat gingerbread mix, muffin mix, half-and-half, eggs, sour cream, molasses, sugar, cinnamon, and nutmeg with an electric mixer on medium speed for 2 minutes. Stir in raisins until combined. Pour batter into prepared slow cooker. Stack 6 paper towels; place over top of slow cooker (to absorb moisture). Secure with lid.

3. Cook on Low heat setting for 2 to 3 hours* or until a wooden tester inserted into center of cake comes out clean. (Do not lift lid for the first 1 hour of cooking.)

4. Run a sharp knife around edge of cake and turn cake out of slow cooker; remove parchment paper. Place on wire rack. Slice and serve warm or at room temperature with ice cream (optional).

*Note: If your slow cooker has "hot spots" and a removable liner, rotate liner every hour of cooking.

Chocolate Coconut Velvet Cake

Prep 25 minutes   **Chill** 3 hours   **Cook** 1½ to 2½ hours (High)   **Makes** 8 servings

1½   cups evaporated milk

¾   cup coconut milk

¼   cup butter

1½   cups dark chocolate chips

1½   cups sifted powdered sugar

¼   cup, plus 3 tablespoons
      cocoa powder

2   teaspoons coconut extract
      Canola oil cooking spray

1   box (18.25-ounce) red velvet
      cake mix

3   eggs

⅓   cup canola oil

3   tablespoons sugar

¾   cup sweetened shredded
      coconut, toasted

1. In a medium saucepan, over medium heat, heat ½ cup of the evaporated milk, ½ cup of the coconut milk, and the butter until butter melts. Stir in chocolate chips, powdered sugar, ¼ cup of the cocoa powder, and the coconut extract until smooth and heated through. Transfer to a medium bowl. Chill until mixture thickens, about 3 hours.*

2. Cut parchment paper to fit the bottom of a 5-quart slow cooker. Coat parchment paper and slow cooker with cooking spray. Set aside.

3. In a large bowl, beat cake mix, the remaining 1 cup evaporated milk, remaining ¼ cup coconut milk, remaining 3 tablespoons cocoa powder, the eggs, oil, and sugar with an electric mixer on low speed for 30 seconds. Scrape down sides of bowl; beat for 2 minutes on medium speed. Pour batter into slow cooker.

4. Scoop half of chocolate mixture by heaping tablespoons over batter in slow cooker. Leave remaining chocolate mixture at room temperature. Stack 6 paper towels; place over top of slow cooker (to absorb moisture). Secure with lid.

5. Cook on High heat setting for 1½ to 2½ hours** or until a wooden tester inserted into center of cake comes out clean. (Do not lift lid for the first 1 hour of cooking.)

6. Turn off slow cooker. If possible, remove liner from slow cooker and place on wire rack. Cool completely before removing cake from slow cooker. Frost cooled cake with remaining chocolate mixture. Garnish with toasted coconut.

*Note: Chocolate mixture can be made a day in advance.

**Note: If your slow cooker has "hot spots" and a removable liner, rotate liner every hour of cooking.

Orange-Glazed Lemon Cake

Prep 15 minutes **Cook** 1 to 1½ hours (High) **Cool** 60 minutes **Makes** 8 servings

Canola oil cooking spray

1 box (15.8-ounce) lemon-poppy seed muffin mix (with lemon glaze pouch*)

¾ cup buttermilk

2 eggs

¼ cup self-rising flour

¼ cup canola oil

3 tablespoons lemonade concentrate

1 can (6.1-ounce) mandarin orange segments, drained (reserve 2 tablespoons juice)

1. Cut parchment paper to fit the bottom of a 5-quart slow cooker. Coat parchment paper and slow cooker with cooking spray. Set aside.

2. In a large bowl, beat muffin mix, buttermilk, eggs, flour, oil, and lemonade concentrate with an electric mixer on medium speed for 2 minutes. Pour batter into prepared slow cooker. Stack 6 paper towels; place over top of slow cooker (to absorb moisture). Secure with lid.

3. Cook on High heat setting for 1 to 1½ hours** or until a wooden tester inserted into center of cake comes out clean. (Do not lift lid for the first 1 hour of cooking.)

4. Run a sharp knife around edge of cake and turn cake out of slow cooker; remove parchment paper. Place on wire rack; cool completely.

5. In a small bowl, stir together contents of lemon glaze pouch and reserved mandarin orange juice until smooth. Drizzle over top of cooled cake. Garnish cake with mandarin orange segments.

*Note: If the muffin mix does not contain a lemon glaze pouch, make a glaze using powdered sugar and reserved mandarin orange juice.

**Note: If your slow cooker has "hot spots" and a removable liner, rotate liner every hour of cooking.

Brownie Bottom Cheesecake

Prep 30 minutes   **Cook** 2½ to 3 hours (High) + 1 to 1½ hours (Low)   **Chill** 4 hours   **Makes** 8 servings

Canola oil cooking spray

1 box (18.3-ounce) fudge brownie mix

4 eggs

⅔ cup canola oil

¼ cup espresso-and-cream coffee drink

2 packages (8 ounces each) cream cheese

⅓ cup sugar

1 tablespoon cake flour

Pinch salt

3 tablespoons heavy cream

1 teaspoon vanilla extract

1. Coat an 8½-inch springform pan with cooking spray. Wrap foil around the bottom of cake pan. Crumple additional aluminum foil to create a "ring base" about 5 inches in diameter and 1 inch thick. Set aside.

2. In a large bowl, stir together brownie mix, two of the eggs, the oil, and coffee drink until combined. Pour into prepared pan.

3. Place foil ring in bottom of slow cooker; pour ½ inch of hot water into bottom of slow cooker. Using 2 long strips of foil, make an "X" over foil ring and bring it up along the sides of slow cooker to assist removing pan from slow cooker. Place springform pan on top of ring and the "X" in slow cooker. Stack 6 paper towels; place over top of slow cooker bowl. Secure with lid.

4. Cook on High heat setting for 1 to 1½ hours. (Do not lift lid for the first 1 hour of cooking.)

5. Meanwhile, in a large bowl, beat cream cheese with an electric mixer on low speed until smooth. Add sugar, flour, and salt; beat until smooth. Add the remaining two eggs, one at a time, beating well after each addition. Scrape down sides of bowl. Add cream and vanilla; beat until combined. Pour over brownie mixture in slow cooker.

6. Cover and cook for 1½ hours more. Turn slow cooker to Low heat setting. Cook for 1 to 1½ hours or until cheesecake is set with a wet-looking center. Turn off heat and let sit, covered, for 30 minutes.

7. Use foil strips to lift springform pan from slow cooker. Place pan on wire rack; let cool to room temperature. Chill in pan for at least 4 hours. Just before serving, remove cake from pan.

Pork and Lamb

Whether they're chops, roast, shoulder, or shanks, pork and lamb will both emerge from the slow cooker succulent and falling-off-the-bone tender. Try homey Gravied Pork Chops and Potatoes for a casual weeknight dinner with the family—or gorgeously glazed Burgundy Lamb Shanks for sit-down-dinner party fare that will wow your guests.

Gravied Pork Chops and Potatoes

Prep 15 minutes   **Cook** 5 to 6 hours (Low)   **Makes** 4 servings

Canola oil cooking spray

1   large onion, sliced

2   pounds potatoes, thinly sliced

4   thick-cut boneless pork chops

Salt and ground black pepper

1   can (10.75-ounce) condensed cream of mushroom soup, *Campbell's*®

½   cup dry sherry

2   teaspoons chopped garlic

1   teaspoon dried sage

1   bay leaf

Chopped fresh flat-leaf parsley (optional)

1. Coat a 4- or 5-quart slow cooker with cooking spray. Place sliced onions in slow cooker. Top with layers of potato slices. Sprinkle pork chops with salt and pepper to taste; place on top of potatoes in slow cooker.

2. In a medium bowl, whisk together mushroom soup, sherry, garlic, sage, and bay leaf until smooth. Pour over pork chops and potatoes in slow cooker.

3. Cover and cook on Low heat setting for 5 to 6 hours.

4. Remove and discard bay leaf. Serve pork chops with potatoes, onions, and cooking juices. Sprinkle with chopped parsley (optional).

Apple-Tea Pork Shoulder

Prep 10 minutes   **Cook** 6 to 8 hours (Low)   **Stand** 10 minutes   **Makes** 8 servings

1	**4-pound boneless pork shoulder roast**
1	**tablespoon olive oil**
6	**cloves garlic, smashed**
1½	**tablespoons chai spice blend**
1	**tablespoon kosher salt**
1	**tablespoon coarsely ground black pepper**
2	**cups chai tea**
1	**cup apple cider**
1	**package (1.3-ounce) roasted pork gravy mix**
1	**bag (20-ounce) frozen roasted potatoes, thawed on cookie sheet**

1. Rub pork roast with olive oil, garlic, spice blend, salt, and pepper. Place roast in a 5-quart slow cooker. In a medium bowl, stir together tea, apple cider, and gravy mix; pour over roast in slow cooker.

2. Cover and cook on Low heat setting for 6 to 8 hours. During the last hour of cooking, add potatoes to slow cooker.

3. Transfer roast to a cutting board; let rest for 10 minutes before slicing. Arrange slices on a serving platter; arrange potatoes around the sliced pork. Spoon gravy over all.

Note: For more flavor, complete Step 1, omitting gravy mix, and marinate roast for 3 to 4 hours in the refrigerator. Stir in gravy mix. Continue as directed.

Rosemary Pork Roast
with Onions

Prep 20 minutes   **Cook** 4 to 5 hours (Low)   **Stand** 10 minutes   **Makes** 4 servings

2   large **Granny Smith apples, peeled, cored, and sliced**

1   large **sweet onion, sliced**

1   2½-**pound boneless pork shoulder roast**

    Salt and ground black pepper

¾   **cup apple jelly**

¼   **cup white wine**

1   **tablespoon dried rosemary**

2   **teaspoons chopped garlic**

1. Place sliced apples and onion slices in a 5-quart slow cooker. Sprinkle roast with salt and pepper to taste; place on top of apples and onions in slow cooker.

2. In a medium bowl, whisk together apple jelly, wine, rosemary, and garlic until combined. Pour over roast in slow cooker.

3. Cover and cook on Low heat setting for 4 to 5 hours.

4. Transfer roast to a cutting board; let rest for 10 minutes before slicing. Using a wire mesh strainer, strain cooking liquid. Skim off any fat from the top of the liquid. Serve sliced roast with apples, onions, and juices.

Creamy Herbed Pork Roast

Prep 20 minutes   **Cook** 6 to 7 hours (Low)   **Makes** 8 servings

2   packages (8 ounces each) sliced fresh mushrooms

1   large onion, sliced

2   cans (10.75 ounces each) condensed cream of mushroom soup, *Campbell's*®

2   teaspoons garlic salt

½   teaspoon dried rosemary

½   teaspoon dried parsley flakes

½   teaspoon dried thyme

1   3½-pound boneless pork loin roast

1. In a 5-quart slow cooker, stir together mushrooms, sliced onion, and 1 can of the mushroom soup until combined.

2. In a small bowl, stir together garlic salt, rosemary, parsley, and thyme. With a sharp knife, score the surface of the pork roast; rub herb mixture into slits. Place roast on top of mushrooms in slow cooker. Spread the remaining can of mushroom soup over top of roast.

3. Cover and cook on Low heat setting for 6 to 7 hours.

4. Transfer roast to a cutting board; let rest for 10 minutes before slicing. Serve sliced roast with mushrooms, onions, and cooking juices.

Chipotle Pork Tacos

Prep 10 minutes   **Cook** 8 to 10 hours (Low)   **Stand** 5 minutes   **Makes** 10 servings

1   3- to 4-pound boneless pork loin roast

1   package (1.25-ounce) taco seasoning mix

1   jar (16-ounce) black bean salsa

2   cans (10 ounces each) black beans, rinsed and drained

2   cubes chipotle bouillon cubes, crushed

1   bottle (12-ounce) beer

1   package (32-ounce) 6-inch corn tortillas

1   package (16-ounce) shredded cheddar cheese

1   medium yellow onion, finely chopped

8   limes, quartered

½   head iceberg lettuce or cabbage, shredded

1   bunch fresh cilantro sprigs

1. Rub pork roast with taco seasoning. Place roast in a 5-quart slow cooker; add salsa and beans. Sprinkle bouillon over all. Add beer; stir to combine.

2. Cover and cook on Low heat setting for 8 to 10 hours.

3. Transfer roast to a serving platter; let rest for 5 minutes, then shred or break up roast with a fork. Using a wire mesh strainer, strain sauce. Pour 1½ cups sauce over shredded pork. Place black beans in serving bowl.

4. Serve shredded pork and the black beans with platters or bowls of warmed tortillas, shredded cheese, chopped onion, lime pieces, shredded lettuce, and cilantro sprigs.

Zesty Lamb Meatballs

Prep 25 minutes   **Cook** 4 to 6 hours (Low)   **Makes** 8 servings

FOR LAMB MEATBALLS:

2	pounds ground lamb
½	cup pita chips, finely crushed
⅓	cup frozen seasoning blend
1	egg
1	tablespoon chopped garlic
1	teaspoon ground cumin

FOR SPICED SAUCE:

1	can (15-ounce) tomato sauce
1	cup Bloody Mary mix
2	tablespoons tomato paste
2	teaspoons ground cinnamon
1	teaspoon ground allspice
1	teaspoon paprika

Hot cooked egg noodles (optional)

1. For lamb meatballs, preheat broiler. Line a baking sheet with aluminum foil; set aside. In a large bowl, mix together ground lamb, crushed pita chips, seasoning blend, egg, garlic, and cumin until well combined.

2. Shape meat mixture into 2-inch balls. Place, evenly spaced, on prepared baking sheet. Broil meatballs 4 to 6 inches from heat for 8 to 10 minutes or until browned, turning once.

3. For spiced sauce, in a large bowl, whisk together tomato sauce, Bloody Mary mix, tomato paste, cinnamon, allspice, and paprika until smooth. Spoon one-fourth of the sauce into a 5-quart slow cooker. Add several meatballs at a time to bowl of sauce, stirring to coat. Transfer coated meatballs to slow cooker. Pour remaining sauce over meatballs in slow cooker.

4. Cover and cook on Low heat setting for 4 to 6 hours.

5. Serve meatballs with sauce on the side or serve meatballs and sauce over hot cooked egg noodles.

Pear and Pearl Lamb Roast

Prep 15 minutes   **Cook** 5 to 7 hours (Low)   **Stand** 10 minutes   **Makes** 6 servings

1	package (14-ounce) frozen petite white pearl onions
1	3½-pound boneless lamb leg roast
12	whole garlic cloves
2	teaspoons Montreal steak seasoning
1	cup beef broth
½	cup pear nectar
½	cup brandy
2	tablespoons tomato paste
2	teaspoons dried fines herbes

1. Place onions in a 5-quart slow cooker. Cut slits in roast with tip of sharp knife; insert whole garlic cloves into slits. Sprinkle roast with steak seasoning; place on top of onions in slow cooker.

2. In a medium bowl, whisk together beef broth, pear nectar, brandy, tomato paste, and fines herbes until combined. Pour over roast in slow cooker.

3. Cover and cook on Low heat setting for 5 to 7 hours.

4. Transfer roast to cutting board; let rest for 10 minutes before slicing. Using a wire mesh strainer, strain sauce into a saucepan. Place onions on serving platter with sliced roast; keep warm. Skim off any fat from the top of the sauce. Bring to a boil over high heat; boil until liquid is reduced by half. Serve sauce with lamb and onions.

Burgundy Lamb Shanks

Prep 20 minutes   **Cook** 10 to 12 hours (Low)   **Makes** 4 servings

4	lamb shanks, trimmed
½	teaspoon fine salt
1	teaspoon freshly ground black pepper
4	medium russet potatoes, quartered
4	yellow onions, quartered
1½	cups Burgundy or Cabernet Sauvignon wine
½	cup balsamic vinegar
12	whole garlic cloves
1	tablespoon chopped garlic
1	packet (1.0-ounce) demi-glace mix
1	teaspoon chopped fresh rosemary
¼	cup unsalted butter, cut into 6 pieces
	Salt and ground black pepper

1. Sprinkle lamb shanks with salt and pepper; set aside.

2. In a 5-quart slow cooker, stir together potatoes, onions, wine, vinegar, garlic cloves, chopped garlic, demi-glace mix, and rosemary until combined. Place lamb shanks on top.

3. Cover and cook on Low heat setting for 10 to 12 hours.

4. Transfer the potatoes to a medium bowl. Using a potato masher, mash potatoes with butter until desired texture. Season to taste with salt and pepper. Serve potatoes with lamb shanks and cooking juices.

Indian-Spiced Lamb Chops

Prep 10 minutes   **Cook** 4 to 6 hours (Low)   **Makes** 4 servings

4	lamb shoulder chops
2	teaspoons Montreal steak seasoning
1½	cups frozen chopped onions
1	can (10.75-ounce) condensed cream of tomato soup, *Campbell's®*
1	cup reduced-sodium chicken broth
¾	cup light coconut milk
2	tablespoons garam masala
1	tablespoon honey
1	tablespoon ginger spice blend
2	tablespoons chopped fresh cilantro leaves

1. Sprinkle chops with steak seasoning; set aside.

2. In a 5-quart slow cooker, stir together onions, tomato soup, chicken broth, coconut milk, garam masala, honey, and ginger until combined. Add lamb chops, pushing them down into the liquid.

3. Cover and cook on Low heat setting for 4 to 6 hours. Remove chops from slow cooker. Sprinkle with cilantro.

Red Wine Shepherd's Pie

Prep 20 minutes   **Cook** 4 to 6 hours (Low)   **Makes** 4 servings

Canola oil cooking spray

1¼   pounds ground lamb

¾   cup frozen chopped onions

3   teaspoons dried rosemary

2   teaspoons chopped garlic

1   can (10.75-ounce) condensed cream of mushroom soup, *Campbell's*®

⅓   cup dry red wine

2   tablespoons mushroom gravy mix

1   bag (16-ounce) frozen petite mixed vegetables

1   container (21-ounce) home-style mashed potatoes

¼   cup garlic-and-herb bread crumbs

1. Coat a 4-quart slow cooker with cooking spray. In a large skillet, over medium heat, cook and stir ground lamb until browned. Drain off fat.

2. In prepared slow cooker, add browned lamb. Stir in onions, 1 teaspoon of the rosemary, and the garlic until combined.

3. In a large bowl, whisk together the remaining 2 teaspoons rosemary, the mushroom soup, wine, and gravy mix. Stir in mixed vegetables until combined. Pour vegetable mixture over lamb in slow cooker.

4. Microwave potatoes in container, uncovered, on high heat setting (100 percent power) for 2 minutes. Stir to loosen. Spread potatoes on top of vegetable mixture in slow cooker. Top with bread crumbs.

5. Cover and cook on Low heat setting for 4 to 6 hours.

Chilies and Stews

I love any dish based on beans. Beans lend themselves to all kinds of great flavors—Southwestern-style chili, Southern-style pintos with bacon, Cuban chili served with saffron rice—and are high in fiber and protein and low in fat. They're tailormade for the slow cooker. And the best part? They feed a crowd for just pennies a person.

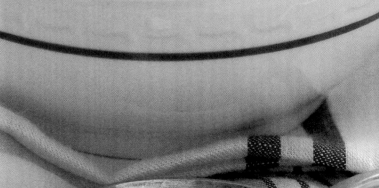

Southwestern Beef and Beans

Prep 20 minutes   **Cook** 4 to 6 hours (High)   **Makes** 6 servings

1   pound lean ground beef

1   pound beef chuck stew meat, cut into bite-size pieces

3   cans (15 ounces each) pinto beans, rinsed and drained

1   jar (16-ounce) hot chunky salsa

1   bag (14-ounce) frozen Southwest vegetable mix

1   can (4-ounce) diced roasted green chile peppers

1   packet (1.25-ounce) Tex-Mex chili seasoning

     Salt and ground black pepper

     Sour cream (optional)

1. In a large skillet, over medium heat, cook and stir ground beef until browned, breaking up clumps. Drain off fat.

2. In a 5-quart slow cooker, stir together browned beef, stew meat, beans, salsa, vegetable mix, chile peppers, and chili seasoning until combined.

3. Cover and cook on High heat setting for 4 to 6 hours. Season to taste with salt and pepper. Top with sour cream (optional).

Cuban Pork and Beans

Prep 10 minutes   **Cook** 6 to 8 hours (Low) + 30 minutes to 1 hour (Low)   **Makes** 8 servings

3   cans (15 ounces each) black beans, rinsed and drained

1   can (14.5-ounce) fire-roasted diced tomatoes

1   cup frozen seasoning blend

2   tablespoons packed brown sugar

2   tablespoons frozen orange juice concentrate

1   tablespoon garlic spice blend

1   tablespoon Key West lime juice

2   teaspoons dried chives

1   2-pound boneless pork shoulder roast

3   tablespoons taco seasoning mix

1. In a 5-quart slow cooker, stir together beans, tomatoes, seasoning blend, brown sugar, orange juice concentrate, garlic spice blend, lime juice, and chives until combined.

2. Sprinkle all sides of pork roast with taco seasoning. Place roast in slow cooker.

3. Cover and cook on Low heat setting for 6 to 8 hours.

4. Transfer roast to a cutting board; let rest for 10 minutes. Shred meat into bite-size pieces; return to slow cooker. Cover and cook another 30 minutes to 1 hour or until heated through.

Country-Style Pintos with Bacon

Prep Overnight + 15 minutes   **Cook** 4 to 6 hours (High)   **Make** 6 servings

1	pound dried pinto beans
½	pound sliced bacon
9	cups vegetable broth
2	teaspoons seasoned salt
1	tablespoon chopped garlic
1	jar (4-ounce) diced pimientos, drained
	Salt and ground black pepper

1. Place beans in a large bowl and cover with water. Soak the beans overnight.*

2. In a medium skillet, over medium heat, fry bacon slices until desired crispness; reserve 2 tablespoons of bacon drippings. Drain bacon slices on paper towels. Crumble bacon; set aside.

3. Drain beans and place in a 5-quart slow cooker. Add vegetable broth. Stir in bacon, the 2 tablespoons reserved bacon drippings, seasoned salt, and garlic.

4. Cover and cook on High heat setting for 4 to 6 hours. During the last 1 hour of cooking, stir in pimientos.

5. Season to taste with salt and pepper. If desired, mash beans with a little bit of cooking liquid before serving.

*Note: Instead of soaking beans overnight, you can "quick soak" them by placing beans in a pot and covering them with at least 2 inches of water. Bring to a boil, turn off heat, and cover pan with lid. Let sit for 1 hour. Drain and use beans in recipe.

Cheesy Chorizo Chili

Prep 15 minutes   **Cook** 5 to 7 hours (Low)   **Makes** 6 servings

8	ounces Mexican chorizo sausage, casing removed
3	cans (15 ounces each) cannellini beans, rinsed and drained
1	can (10.75-ounce) condensed cheddar cheese soup, *Campbell's®*
1	can (10-ounce) diced tomatoes with lime juice and cilantro
1	can (7-ounce) diced mild green chiles
1	tablespoon, plus 1 teaspoon fajita seasoning
1	teaspoon cumin
1	teaspoon chili powder
½	teaspoon ground chipotle chile pepper
	Salt and ground black pepper
	Shredded Mexican cheese blend
	Finely chopped scallions (green onions)

1. In a large skillet, over medium heat, cook and stir chorizo until browned, breaking up clumps. Drain on paper towels.

2. In a 5-quart slow cooker, stir together chorizo, beans, cheese soup, tomatoes, chiles, fajita seasoning, cumin, chili powder, and ground chipotle until combined.

3. Cover and cook on Low heat setting for 5 to 7 hours.

4. Season to taste with salt and pepper. Spoon into soup bowls. Top with shredded cheese and scallions.

Caribbean Chili

Prep 10 minutes   **Cook** 4 to 6 hours (High)   **Makes** 6 servings

1   package (10-ounce) linguica sausage links, quartered lengthwise and chopped

1   jar (16-ounce) black bean and corn salsa

1   can (15.25-ounce) kidney beans, rinsed and drained

1   can (15-ounce) black beans, rinsed and drained

1   bag (8-ounce) precut butternut squash, cut into bite-size pieces

1   cup frozen chopped green peppers

1   container (5-ounce) diced onions

½   cup vegetable broth

1½   teaspoons chopped garlic

1   teaspoon Caribbean jerk seasoning

1   teaspoon paprika

     Salt and ground black pepper

     Hot cooked saffron rice (optional)

1. In a 5-quart slow cooker, stir together sausage, salsa, all beans, squash, green peppers, onions, vegetable broth, garlic, jerk seasoning, and paprika until combined. Season to taste with salt and black pepper.

2. Cover and cook on High heat setting for 4 to 6 hours.

3. Serve over saffron rice (optional).

New Orleans Red Beans

Prep 10 minutes   **Cook** 4 to 6 hours (High)   **Makes** 8 servings

1   package (13-ounce) **Cajun-style andouille sausage, diced**

1   **pound smoked ham steak, diced**

3   **cans (15 ounces each) kidney beans, rinsed and drained**

2   **cups spicy vegetable juice**

1¼   **cups frozen seasoning blend**

1   **tablespoon Worcestershire sauce**

1   **tablespoon chopped garlic**

2   **teaspoons Cajun seasoning**

1   **bay leaf**

    Hot cooked instant rice

    Hot pepper sauce (optional)

1. In a 5-quart slow cooker, stir together sausage, ham, beans, vegetable juice, seasoning blend, Worcestershire sauce, garlic, and Cajun seasoning until combined. Add bay leaf.

2. Cover and cook on High heat setting for 4 to 6 hours.

3. Remove and discard bay leaf. Serve red beans over hot cooked rice. Serve with hot pepper sauce (optional).

Santa Fe Mole Chili

Prep 15 minutes   **Cook** 6 to 8 hours (Low)   **Makes** 6 servings

1   **pound ground chicken**

3   **cans (15 ounces each) pinto beans, rinsed and drained**

1   **can (10-ounce) diced tomatoes and green chiles**

¾   **cup frozen chopped onions**

¼   **cup sliced jalapeños**

1   **teaspoon chili powder**

¼   **cup mole paste**

¾   **cup chicken broth**

    Salt and ground black pepper

    Shredded Mexican cheese blend (optional)

1. In a large skillet, over medium heat, cook and stir ground chicken until browned, breaking up clumps. Drain off fat.

2. In a 5-quart slow cooker, stir together browned chicken, beans, tomatoes, onions, jalapeños, and chili powder until combined. In a medium microwave-safe bowl, stir together mole paste and chicken broth. Microwave on high heat setting (100 percent power) for 1 to 2 minutes or until paste starts to dissolve. Whisk until combined; stir into slow cooker.

3. Cover and cook on Low heat setting for 6 to 8 hours.

4. Season to taste with salt and pepper. Spoon into soup bowls. Sprinkle with shredded cheese (optional).

Hawaiian Honey Chili

Prep 15 minutes   **Cook** 4 to 6 hours (High)   **Makes** 6 servings

1¼   pounds ground chicken

1   can (20-ounce) pineapple chunks in juice, drained (reserve ½ cup juice)

¼   cup soy sauce

3   tablespoons white chicken chili seasoning

2   tablespoons honey

2   teaspoons chopped garlic

¾   teaspoon ground ginger

½   teaspoon ground cloves

1¼   cups chopped sweet onion

1   can (15-ounce) white beans, rinsed and drained

1   can (14.5-ounce) diced tomatoes with green peppers and onions

2   tablespoons diced jalapeños

Salt and ground black pepper

1. In a large skillet, over medium heat, cook and stir ground chicken until browned, breaking up clumps. Drain off fat. Place chicken in a 5-quart slow cooker.

2. In a small bowl, stir together pineapple chunks, reserved pineapple juice, soy sauce, the chili seasoning, honey, garlic, ginger, and cloves until combined. Pour into slow cooker. Stir in onion, beans, tomatoes, and jalapeños.

3. Cover and cook on High heat setting for 4 to 6 hours. Season to taste with salt and black pepper.

Italian Sausage and White Beans

Prep 10 minutes   **Cook** 4 to 6 hours (High)   **Makes** 8 servings

2   packages (13 ounces each) garlic and artichoke sausages

3   cans (15 ounces each) white beans

1   can (14.5-ounce) petite diced tomatoes

1   cup frozen chopped onions

1   cup red wine

⅓   cup crumbled cooked bacon

1   teaspoon Italian seasoning

1   teaspoon chopped garlic

½   teaspoon freshly ground black pepper

Salt and ground black pepper

1. Cut sausages diagonally into 1-inch-thick slices. In a 5-quart slow cooker, stir together sausages, beans, tomatoes, onions, wine, bacon, Italian seasoning, garlic, and pepper until combined.

2. Cover and cook on High heat setting for 4 to 6 hours. Season to taste with salt and pepper.

Turkey-Chicken Chili

Prep 15 minutes　　**Cook** 4 to 6 hours (High)　　**Makes** 6 servings

1¼	pounds ground turkey
2	cans (15 ounces each) kidney beans
1	jar (26-ounce) marinara sauce
1	can (10-ounce) chili fixin's
1	can (9.75-ounce) chicken breast packed in water
½	cup frozen chopped onions
1	packet (1.25-ounce) chili seasoning
1	tablespoon packed brown sugar
	Salt and ground black pepper
	Shredded cheddar cheese (optional)

1. In a large skillet, over medium heat, cook and stir ground turkey until browned, breaking up clumps. Drain off fat.

2. In a 5-quart slow cooker, stir together browned turkey, beans, marinara sauce, chili fixin's, chicken, onions, chili seasoning, and brown sugar until combined.

3. Cover and cook on High heat setting for 4 to 6 hours.

4. Season to taste with salt and pepper. Spoon into soup bowls. Sprinkle with shredded cheese (optional).

Pasta and Sauces

Everyone loves noodles and sauce any night of the week, whether it's spaghetti with meat sauce, ravioli, or creamy Swedish meatballs with fettuccine. Those traditionally slow-simmered stovetop sauces are perfect for the slow cooker. Even rich layered lasagna translates beautifully to this terrific appliance. Try my Hot Italian Sausage Lasagna (page 152) or 5-Cheese Pesto Lasagna (page 154) to see for yourself!

Sweet Italian Meatball Pasta

Prep 25 minutes **Cook** 3 to 4 hours (Low) **Makes** 8 servings

FOR MEATBALLS:

½	pound ground beef
8	ounces bulk sweet Italian sausage, *Johnsonville®*
¼	cup frozen seasoning blend
1	egg
3	tablespoons Italian-style bread crumbs
2	teaspoons dried Italian seasoning
2	teaspoons chopped garlic
1 ½	teaspoons hamburger seasoning

FOR PASTA AND SAUCE:

	Canola oil cooking spray
1	jar (24-ounce) Cabernet marinara sauce
2	cups beef broth
1 ½	cups water
1	pound dried gemelli pasta
	Shredded Parmesan cheese (optional)

1. For meatballs, preheat broiler. Line 2 baking sheets with aluminum foil; set aside. In a large bowl, mix together ground beef, sausage, seasoning blend, egg, bread crumbs, Italian seasoning, garlic, and hamburger seasoning until well combined.

2. Shape meat mixture into 1-inch balls. Place, evenly spaced, on prepared baking sheets. Broil meatballs 4 to 6 inches from heat for 8 to 10 minutes or until browned, turning once.

3. For pasta and sauce, coat a 5-quart slow cooker with cooking spray. Pour marinara sauce, beef broth, and water into slow cooker. Add meatballs and gemelli pasta; carefully stir until combined.

4. Cover and cook on Low heat setting for 3 to 4 hours. Sprinkle with Parmesan cheese (optional).

Beefy Cheesy Ravioli

Prep 20 minutes   **Cook** 3 to 4 hours (High)   **Makes** 6 servings

Canola oil cooking spray

2   jars (26 ounces each) pasta sauce
    with meat

1   can (14.5-ounce) diced tomatoes
    with basil, garlic, and oregano

1   can (10.75-ounce) condensed
    cheddar cheese soup, *Campbell's*®

2   teaspoons chopped garlic

1   bag (25-ounce) frozen beef ravioli,
    not thawed

1   cup shredded Parmesan cheese

1   cup shredded mozzarella cheese

1. Coat a 5-quart slow cooker with cooking spray. In a large bowl, stir together pasta sauce, tomatoes, cheese soup, and garlic until combined. Spoon one-third of the sauce into slow cooker; top with one-third of the ravioli. Sprinkle ⅓ cup each of Parmesan and mozzarella cheeses over ravioli. Repeat layers 2 more times.

2. Cover and cook on High heat setting for 3 to 4 hours.

Creamy Swedish Meatball Fettuccine

Prep 10 minutes   **Cook** 2 to 3 hours (High)   **Makes** 10 servings

Canola oil cooking spray

2   pounds fully cooked frozen meatballs

1   cup frozen chopped onions

1   can (10.5-ounce) white sauce

1   cup beef broth

1   packet (1.5-ounce) beef stroganoff
    seasoning mix

2   tablespoons chopped garlic

1   tablespoon Worcestershire sauce

1   cup sour cream

    Hot cooked fettuccine

1. Coat a 5-quart slow cooker with cooking spray. In slow cooker, stir together meatballs and onions until combined. In a large bowl, whisk together white sauce, beef broth, seasoning mix, garlic, and Worcestershire sauce until smooth; pour over meatballs in slow cooker.

2. Cover and cook on High heat setting for 2 to 3 hours.

3. Just before serving, stir in sour cream. Serve meatballs over hot cooked fettuccine.

Fiesta Mac 'n' Cheese

Prep 10 minutes   **Cook** 2½ to 3½ hours (Low)   **Makes** 6 servings

Canola oil cooking spray

2 cans (10 ounces each) condensed cheddar cheese soup, *Campbell's*®

3 cups water

2¼ cups reduced-sodium beef broth

2 tablespoons Tex-Mex chili seasoning mix

2 teaspoons chopped garlic

1 container (18-ounce) shredded beef in barbecue sauce

1 box (16-ounce) dried elbow macaroni

2 cups shredded Mexican cheese blend

¾ cup frozen seasoning blend

1 can (7-ounce) diced mild green chiles

Salt and ground black pepper

1. Coat a 5-quart slow cooker with cooking spray. In slow cooker, whisk together cheese soup, water, beef broth, seasoning mix, and garlic until smooth. Add shredded beef, macaroni, cheese blend, seasoning blend, and chiles; stir until combined.

2. Cover and cook on Low heat setting for 2½ to 3½ hours. Season to taste with salt and black pepper.

Spaghetti with White Wine Bolognese

Prep 15 minutes   **Cook** 8 to 9 hours (Low) + 30 minutes (High)   **Makes** 8 servings

1   pound ground pork

1   pound lean ground beef

1   pound ground veal

1   can (28-ounce) whole peeled tomatoes with basil, cut up

1   can (15-ounce) Italian-style tomato sauce

1   cup reduced-sodium beef broth

1   cup evaporated milk

1   cup Chardonnay or other white wine

1   cup frozen chopped onions

1   cup finely chopped celery and carrot sticks

2   tablespoons chopped garlic

Hot cooked spaghetti

Grated Parmesan cheese (optional)

1. In a large skillet, over medium heat, cook and stir all ground meat until browned, breaking up clumps. Drain off fat.

2. In a 5-quart slow cooker, stir together browned meat, tomatoes, tomato sauce, beef broth, evaporated milk, wine, onions, celery and carrots, and garlic until combined.

3. Cover and cook on Low heat setting for 8 to 9 hours.

4. Thirty minutes before serving, remove lid and turn slow cooker to High heat setting to help thicken sauce. Skim any fat from top of sauce. Serve over hot cooked spaghetti. Sprinkle with Parmesan cheese (optional).

Peppered Pork and Caper Bow Ties

Prep 15 minutes   **Cook** 8 to 9 hours (Low) + 30 minutes (High)   **Makes** 8 servings

1   3-pound boneless pork shoulder roast, cut into bite-size pieces

1   can (28-ounce) Italian-style crushed tomatoes

1   jar (26-ounce) tomato-and-basil pasta sauce

1   cup vegetable broth

1   cup frozen chopped onions

1   jar (6-ounce) pitted kalamata olives, drained and chopped

⅓   cup capers, drained

1   can (2-ounce) anchovy fillets, minced

2   tablespoons chopped garlic

1½   teaspoons red pepper flakes

     Hot cooked bow tie pasta

1. In a 5-quart slow cooker, stir together pork, tomatoes, pasta sauce, vegetable broth, onions, olives, capers, anchovies, garlic, and red pepper flakes until combined.

2. Cover and cook on Low heat setting for 8 to 9 hours.

3. Thirty minutes before serving, remove lid and turn slow cooker to High heat setting to help thicken sauce. Serve over hot cooked bow tie pasta.

Cheesy Sausage Tortellini

Prep 10 minutes   **Cook** 2½ to 3½ hours (High)   **Makes** 6 servings

Canola oil cooking spray

1   can (28-ounce) whole peeled tomatoes with basil, cut up

1   package (16-ounce) Italian sausage links, *Johnsonville*®

1   can (14-ounce) vegetable broth

1   can (10.75-ounce) condensed tomato soup, *Campbell's*®

3   tablespoons tomato paste

1   tablespoon basil-and-garlic seasoning blend

2   packages (8 ounces each) three-cheese tortellini

1½   cups shredded mozzarella cheese

1. Coat a 4-quart slow cooker with cooking spray. Place tomatoes and sausage in slow cooker; set aside.

2. In a large bowl, whisk together vegetable broth, tomato soup, tomato paste, and seasoning blend until smooth. Pour into slow cooker; stir until combined.

3. Cover and cook on High heat setting for 2½ to 3½ hours. During the last 30 minutes of cooking time, stir in tortellini.

4. Turn off slow cooker. Sprinkle mozzarella cheese over top of sausage mixture, cover, and let sit until cheese melts.

Hot Italian Sausage Lasagna

Prep 30 minutes   **Cook** 3 to 4 hours (Low)   **Makes** 8 servings

1   package (16-ounce) hot Italian
     sausage links, *Johnsonville*®

1   container (15-ounce) ricotta
     cheese

1   cup shredded Italian cheese blend

1   egg

2½   teaspoons dried Italian seasoning

     Salt and ground black pepper

2   cups frozen yellow and green
     zucchini squash, thawed

¾   cup sliced roasted red bell peppers

¼   cup pine nuts

     Canola oil cooking spray

2   jars (24 ounces each) marinara
     with mushroom pasta sauce

1   box (9-ounce) no-boil lasagna
     noodles

1   package (8-ounce) sliced
     provolone cheese

1. In a large skillet, over medium heat, brown all sides of sausages. Remove from skillet and cut into ¼-inch slices; set aside.

2. In a medium bowl, stir together ricotta cheese, cheese blend, egg, Italian seasoning, and salt and black pepper to taste until combined; set aside. In a medium bowl, toss together squash, roasted peppers, and pine nuts; set aside.

3. Coat a 5-quart slow cooker with cooking spray. Pour ½ cup of the pasta sauce into slow cooker. Top with a layer of lasagna noodles, breaking them to fit. Layer one-third of the sausage, one-third of the ricotta mixture, one-third of the squash mixture, and one-third of provolone slices over noodles. Top provolone with 1 cup of the pasta sauce. Repeat layers 2 more times. Finish with noodles and the remaining pasta sauce on top.

4. Cover and cook on Low heat setting for 3 to 4 hours.

5-Cheese Pesto Lasagna

Prep 30 minutes   **Cook** 3 to 4 hours (Low)   **Stand** 10 minutes   **Makes** 8 servings

Canola oil cooking spray

1 pound ground chicken

1 cup diced onions

1 container (7-ounce) refrigerated pesto sauce

1 box (10-ounce) frozen chopped spinach, thawed and squeezed dry

1 container (8-ounce) mascarpone cheese, softened

1 cup ricotta cheese

1 cup grated Parmesan cheese

1 egg

2 jars (16 ounces each) Alfredo sauce

1 box (9-ounce) no-boil lasagna noodles

1 package (8-ounce) sliced provolone cheese

4 cups shredded mozzarella cheese

1. Coat a 5-quart slow cooker with cooking spray; set aside.

2. In a large skillet, over medium heat, cook and stir ground chicken until browned, breaking up clumps. Drain off fat. Remove from heat; stir in onions and pesto. Set aside.

3. In a medium bowl, stir together spinach, mascarpone cheese, ricotta cheese, Parmesan cheese, and egg until combined; set aside.

4. Pour ¾ cup of the Alfredo sauce into slow cooker. Top with a layer of lasagna noodles, breaking them to fit. Spread one-third of the ricotta mixture over noodles. Layer one-third of the chicken mixture, 4 slices provolone, and 1 cup mozzarella cheese over ricotta layer. Repeat layers two more times. Finish with noodles and the remaining Alfredo sauce on top.

5. Cover and cook on Low heat setting for 3 to 4 hours or until noodles are tender.

6. Turn off slow cooker. Sprinkle the remaining 1 cup mozzarella cheese over top of lasagna, cover, and let sit until cheese melts.

Creamy Chicken Manicotti

Prep 25 minutes   **Cook** 2½ to 3½ hours (Low)   **Makes** 6 servings

2   jars (16 ounces each) Alfredo sauce

1   can (14-ounce) chicken broth

2   packages (6 ounces each) grilled chicken breast strips, finely chopped

1¼   cups frozen petite peas, thawed

1   cup ricotta cheese

4   ounces cream cheese, softened

¼   cup refrigerated pesto sauce

1   box (8-ounce) dried manicotti pasta shells

        Canola oil cooking spray

1   cup shredded Italian cheese blend

        Chopped fresh flat-leaf parsley (optional)

1. In a medium bowl, whisk together Alfredo sauce and chicken broth until smooth; set aside. In a second medium bowl, stir together chicken, peas, ricotta cheese, cream cheese, and pesto until combined. Fill dried manicotti shells with chicken mixture.

2. Coat a 5-quart slow cooker with cooking spray. Pour one-third of the Alfredo sauce into slow cooker. Fit half of the filled shells in bottom of slow cooker; top with another one-third of the Alfredo sauce. Sprinkle ½ cup of the cheese blend over top. Repeat with the remaining filled shells, the remaining one-third of the Alfredo sauce, and the remaining ½ cup of the cheese blend.

3. Cover and cook on Low heat setting for 2½ to 3½ hours. Sprinkle with chopped parsley (optional).

Black Olive and Mushroom Penne

Prep 10 minutes　　**Cook** 2½ to 3 hours (High)　　**Makes** 6 servings

Canola oil cooking spray

2　packages (8 ounces each) sliced fresh brown mushrooms

1　can (6-ounce) medium pitted black olives, drained

2　cups evaporated milk

2　cups chicken broth

1　can (10.75-ounce) condensed cream of mushroom soup, Campbell's®

1　packet (1.5-ounce) four-cheese sauce mix

2　teaspoons dried Italian seasoning

Salt and ground black pepper

1　box (16-ounce) dried penne pasta

Shredded Parmesan cheese (optional)

1. Coat a 5-quart slow cooker with cooking spray. Place mushrooms and olives in slow cooker. In a large bowl, whisk together evaporated milk, chicken broth, mushroom soup, sauce mix, Italian seasoning, and salt and pepper to taste until combined. Pour into slow cooker.

2. Cover and cook on High heat setting for 2½ to 3 hours. During last 40 minutes of cooking time, stir in pasta. Sprinkle with Parmesan (optional).

Garlic-Vodka Angel Hair

Prep 10 minutes　　**Cook** 8 to 10 hours (Low) + 30 minutes (High)　　**Makes** 6 servings

2　cans (28 ounces each) Italian-style diced tomatoes

1　can (6-ounce) tomato paste

1　container (5-ounce) diced onions

½　cup vodka

3　tablespoons chopped garlic

1　tablespoon dried Italian seasoning

¾　cup half-and-half

Salt and ground black pepper

Hot cooked angel hair pasta

Fresh basil leaves (optional)

1. In a 4-quart slow cooker, stir together tomatoes, tomato paste, onions, vodka, garlic, and Italian seasoning until combined.

2. Cover and cook on Low heat setting for 8 to 10 hours.

3. Thirty minutes before serving, remove lid and turn slow cooker to High heat setting to help thicken sauce. Stir in half-and-half. Season with salt and pepper. Serve over hot cooked angel hair pasta. Top with basil leaves (optional).

One-Pot Meals

The convenience of a one-dish dinner is undeniable. And when it's made in the slow cooker, it's even better because it's ready to eat when you are. These one-pot meals hold a world of flavors. From Lamb with Ratatouille to Cajun Shrimp and Rice to Moroccan-inspired Sweet Potato Turkey Bowl, there is something to suit every mood.

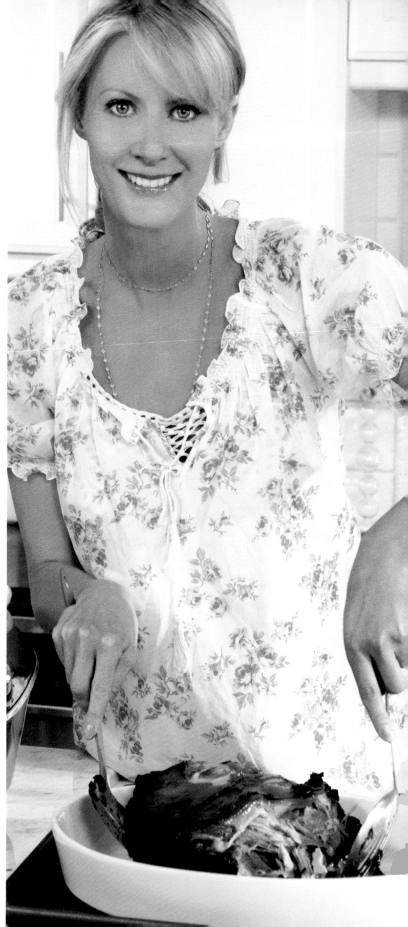

Pumpkin Pie Brisket

Prep 15 minutes **Cook** 23 to 24 hours (Low) **Stand** 10 minutes **Makes** 6 servings

1	sweet onion, sliced ½ inch thick
1	4-pound beef brisket, trimmed
1	envelope (1-ounce) golden onion soup mix
½	cup bourbon
1	tablespoon Worcestershire sauce
3	cups frozen chopped collard greens
¾	cup apricot preserves
¼	cup orange juice
1	teaspoon pumpkin pie spice
2	sweet potatoes, peeled and cut into 1-inch cubes

1. Place onion slices in the bottom of a 5-quart slow cooker. Sprinkle brisket with onion soup mix; place in slow cooker, flat side up, on top of onions. (If necessary, cut brisket to fit.)

2. In a small bowl, stir together bourbon and Worcestershire sauce until combined. Pour over brisket in slow cooker.

3. Cover and cook on Low heat setting for 21 hours.

4. Remove lid and add collard greens to slow cooker, placing them around and underneath brisket. In a large microwave-safe bowl, combine apricot preserves, orange juice, and pumpkin pie spice. Microwave on high heat setting (100 percent power) for 1 minute; stir until smooth. Add sweet potatoes; toss to coat. Place sweet potatoes on top of brisket in slow cooker.

5. Cover and cook on Low heat setting for 2 to 3 hours more.

6. Transfer brisket to a cutting board; let rest for 10 minutes before slicing. Serve sliced brisket with sweet potatoes and collard greens.

Florentine Pot Roast

Prep 15 minutes   **Cook** 8 to 10 hours (Low)   **Makes** 6 servings

1   pound whole baby red-skinned potatoes, halved

1   large onion, quartered

1   3-pound beef chuck roast

1   tablespoon dried rosemary

1   can (10-ounce) condensed cream of mushroom soup, *Campbell's*®

1   packet (1.5-ounce) beef stew seasoning mix

1   tablespoon chopped garlic

1   package (8-ounce) sliced fresh mushrooms

1   can (28-ounce) Italian stewed tomatoes, cut up

1. In a 5- to 6-quart slow cooker, combine potatoes and onion. Sprinkle both sides of roast with rosemary. Place meat on top of vegetables in slow cooker.

2. In a small bowl, stir together mushroom soup, stew seasoning mix, and garlic in a small bowl. Pour over roast in slow cooker. Top with mushrooms and tomatoes.

3. Cover and cook on Low heat setting for 8 to 10 hours.

Rich Ranch Beef Roast

Prep 15 minutes   **Cook** 5 to 6 hours (Low)   **Stand** 10 minutes   **Makes** 6 servings

1   pound baby Yukon gold potatoes (cut large potatoes in half)

6   mini ears of corn on the cob

1   3-pound boneless beef chuck roast

2   tablespoons ranch dip mix

3   cups frozen cut green beans

1   medium sweet onion, sliced

1   jar (12-ounce) beef gravy

1   tablespoon Worcestershire sauce

½   cup crumbled cooked bacon

1. In a 5- to 6-quart slow cooker, combine potatoes and corn. Sprinkle both sides of roast with ranch dip mix. Place roast on top of vegetables in slow cooker. Top meat with green beans and onion slices.

2. In a small bowl, stir together gravy and Worcestershire sauce. Pour over steak and vegetables in slow cooker. Sprinkle bacon over top.

3. Cover and cook on Low heat setting for 5 to 6 hours.

4. Transfer roast to a cutting board; let rest for 10 minutes before slicing. Serve sliced roast with vegetables.

Apple-Spice Skirt Steak

Prep 15 minutes   **Cook** 5 to 6 hours (Low)   **Makes** 6 servings

2   cans (14 ounces each) beef broth

1   can (14.5-ounce) diced tomatoes with onions and green peppers

½   pound baby Yukon gold potatoes, quartered

1   cup coconut milk

1   cup frozen sliced carrots

1   cup frozen peas

1   cup frozen chopped onions

1   Granny Smith apple, peeled, cored, and chopped

¾   cup converted rice

1   tablespoon curry powder

½   cup golden raisins

1   1½-pound skirt steak

2   teaspoons garam masala

    Salt and ground black pepper

1. In a 5-quart slow cooker, stir together beef broth, tomatoes, potatoes, coconut milk, carrots, peas, onions, apple, rice, curry powder, and raisins until combined. Sprinkle all sides of skirt steak with garam masala and salt and pepper to taste. Place steak on top of vegetables and rice in slow cooker.

2. Cover and cook on Low heat setting for 5 to 6 hours.

3. Transfer steak to a cutting board and slice across the grain. Serve steak with rice mixture.

Mom's Meat Loaf Meal

Prep 25 minutes   **Cook** 1 hour (High) + 5 to 6 hours (Low)   **Makes** 6 servings

1½   pounds red potatoes, finely chopped

1   packet (0.6-ounce) Italian salad dressing mix

1¼   pounds lean ground beef

1   pound hot Italian sausage, casings removed, *Johnsonville*®

1   package (3-ounce) prosciutto, finely chopped

1   can (10.75-ounce) condensed tomato soup, *Campbell's*®

1   jar (6.5-ounce) marinated artichoke hearts, drained, chopped

⅓   cup Italian bread crumbs

¼   cup refrigerated pesto sauce

1   egg

1   can (10.75-ounce) condensed cream of mushroom with roasted garlic soup, *Campbell's*®

½   cup beef broth

2   cups frozen pepper strips, chopped

1   onion, chopped

    Prepared frozen garlic bread

1. In a 5-quart slow cooker, toss together potatoes with half of the Italian dressing mix until coated; set aside.

2. In a large bowl, mix together ground beef, sausage, proscuitto, ¼ cup of the tomato soup, the artichoke hearts, bread crumbs, pesto, and egg until well combined. Shape beef mixture into a loaf; place loaf in slow cooker on top of potatoes. (Make sure meat loaf does not touch the sides of the slow cooker.)

3. In a small bowl, stir together the remaining tomato soup, the mushroom soup, and beef broth until combined. Pour over meat loaf. In a medium bowl, toss together peppers and onions with remaining Italian dressing mix until coated. Place on top of meat loaf in slow cooker.

4. Cover and cook on High heat setting for 1 hour. Turn to Low heat setting. Cook for 5 to 6 hours more.

5. Transfer meat loaf to a cutting board. Slice meat loaf and serve with potatoes, peppers, and onion. Serve with prepared garlic bread.

Cajun Pork Chops

Prep 10 minutes   **Cook** 4 to 5 hours (Low)   **Makes** 6 servings

3½   cups vegetable broth

1½   cups converted rice

6   thick center-cut pork chops

1   tablespoon seafood seasoning

2   cans (10.7 ounces each) condensed cream of celery soup, *Campbell's*®

2   cups frozen chopped green peppers

2   cups frozen chopped onions

1   packet (1-ounce) onion soup mix

1   tablespoon Cajun seasoning

1. In a 5-quart slow cooker, stir together vegetable broth and rice until combined. Sprinkle both sides of pork chops with seafood seasoning. Place chops on top of rice in the slow cooker.

2. In a large bowl, stir together celery soup, peppers, onions, soup mix, and Cajun seasoning until combined. Pour over chops in slow cooker.

3. Cover and cook on Low heat setting for 4 to 5 hours.

Pork Tenderloin
with Sauerkraut and Sausages

Prep 15 minutes   **Cook** 5 to 6 hours (Low)   **Makes** 6 servings

2   cups sauerkraut

1   cup frozen chopped onions

1   cup baby carrots, cut in ½-inch pieces

½   cup pearl barley

1   pound bratwurst sausages, cut in half, *Johnsonville®*

2   pounds pork tenderloin, cut into bite-size pieces

1   envelope (1-ounce) golden onion soup mix

2   cups reduced-sodium beef broth

1   bottle (12-ounce) beer

1   can (10.75-ounce) condensed cream of mushroom soup with roasted garlic, *Campbell's®*

1. In a 5-quart slow cooker, stir together sauerkraut, onions, carrots, and barley until combined. Sprinkle bratwurst and pork with soup mix. Place on top of vegetables in slow cooker.

2. In a large bowl, whisk together beef broth, beer, and mushroom soup until smooth. Pour over meat in slow cooker.

3. Cover and cook on Low heat setting for 5 to 6 hours.

Tender Gravied Pork Roast

Prep 20 minutes   **Cook** 7 to 8 hours (Low)   **Stand** 10 minutes   **Makes** 6 servings

1	**3-pound boneless pork loin, tied crosswise at 1-inch intervals***
2	**teaspoons ground black pepper**
1	**teaspoon dried oregano leaves**
1	**teaspoon salt**
2	**packages (8 ounces each) whole cremini mushrooms**
1	**package (16-ounce) frozen corn cobettes, thawed, cut in half**
1	**bag (12-ounce) frozen chopped onions**
2	**cans beef consommé**
1	**cup frozen tamarind paste,** thawed**
2	**cubes chipotle bouillon cubes, crumbled**
3	**tablespoons sugar**
3	**tablespoons cornstarch**
3	**tablespoons water**

1. Rub the pork with pepper, oregano, and salt. Place the meat in a 5-quart slow cooker. Add mushrooms, corn, and onions to the slow cooker.

2. In a medium microwave-safe bowl, combine the consommé, tamarind paste, bouillon cubes, and sugar. Microwave on high setting (100 percent power) for 2 to 3 minutes; stir. Using a wire mesh strainer, strain mixture into the slow cooker, scraping the inside of the strainer to get as much pulp (but no fibers) into the pot as possible.

3. Cover and cook on Low heat setting for 7 to 8 hours.

4. Transfer meat to a cutting board; let stand for 10 minutes before slicing. Remove and discard string from pork; slice pork.

5. Pour cooking liquid into a medium saucepan; bring to a boil over medium-high heat. In a small bowl, stir together cornstarch and water; whisk into saucepan. Reduce heat; simmer for 3 to 4 minutes or until sauce is thickened. Serve pork with vegetables and sauce.

*Note: Ask the butcher to tie the pork loin for you.

**Note: If you can't find tamarind paste at your supermarket, scrape off the pulp from about 10 to 12 fresh pods.

Lamb with Ratatouille

Prep 25 minutes   **Cook** 7 to 8 hours (Low)   **Makes** 6 servings

1	large onion, sliced
1	medium eggplant, chopped
1½	cups yellow and green zucchini squash
2	cups frozen pepper strips
1	can (28-ounce) crushed tomatoes with roasted garlic
2	tablespoons Montreal steak seasoning
3	teaspoons herbes de Provence
1	teaspoon garlic salt
1	3-pound boneless lamb leg roast
2	tablespoons extra virgin olive oi
1	can (14-ounce) beef broth
½	cup red wine
2	tablespoons tomato paste

1. In a 5- to 6-quart slow cooker, layer onion slices, eggplant, squash, pepper strips, and tomatoes.

2. In a small bowl, stir together steak seasoning, 2 teaspoons of the herbes de Provence, and the garlic salt. Rub spice mixture all over lamb. In a large skillet, heat oil over medium-high heat. Brown all sides of lamb in hot oil. Place browned lamb on top of vegetables in slow cooker.

3. In a medium bowl, whisk together beef broth, wine, tomato paste, and the remaining 1 teaspoon herbes de Provence until combined. Pour over lamb and vegetables in slow cooker.

4. Cover and cook on Low heat setting for 7 to 8 hours.

5. Transfer lamb to a cutting board; let rest for 10 minutes before cutting into chunks. Stir vegetable mixture and serve with lamb.

Marmalade Chicken and Vegetables

Prep 15 minutes   **Cook** 3 to 4 hours (Low)   **Stand** 5 minutes   **Makes** 4 servings

1   package (16-ounce) diced red potatoes

1   large onion, chopped

1   cup frozen diced green peppers

¼   cup chopped roasted red peppers

4   boneless skinless chicken breasts

1½   teaspoons lemon pepper

½   teaspoon kosher salt

1   cup marmalade

½   cup chicken broth

¼   cup dry white wine

¼   cup butter

1   box (6-ounce) corn bread stuffing mix

1. In a 5-quart slow cooker, stir together potatoes, onion, green peppers, and roasted peppers. Sprinkle both sides of chicken with lemon pepper and salt. Place chicken on top of vegetables. In a bowl, whisk together marmalade, chicken broth, and wine. Pour over chicken and vegetables.

2. Cover and cook on Low heat setting for 3 to 4 hours.

3. Transfer chicken and vegetables to a platter; keep warm. Pour cooking liquid and enough water to equal 1½ cups into a medium saucepan. Add butter and bring to a boil. Stir in stuffing mix; remove from heat. Let sit for 5 minutes. Fluff stuffing with a fork. Serve with chicken and vegetables.

Chicken Broccoli Mac 'n' Cheese

Prep 15 minutes   **Cook** 3½ to 4½ hours (Low)   **Makes** 6 servings

Canola oil cooking spray

3   cups chicken broth

1   can (10.75-ounce) condensed cream of broccoli soup, *Campbell's*®

1   cup evaporated milk

1   packet (1.5-ounce) four-cheese sauce mix

12   ounces dried elbow macaroni

2   cups shredded sharp cheddar cheese

1¼   pounds ground chicken

4   cups fresh broccoli florets

1   cup frozen seasoning blend

1   tablespoon chopped garlic

1. Coat a 5-quart slow cooker with cooking spray; set aside.

2. In a large bowl, whisk together chicken broth, broccoli soup, milk, and cheese sauce mix until smooth. Stir in macaroni and cheddar cheese until combined; pour into prepared slow cooker. In a large skillet, over medium heat, cook and stir ground chicken until browned, breaking up clumps. Drain off fat. Remove from heat; stir in broccoli, seasoning blend, and garlic until combined. Add to slow cooker; stir to combine.

3. Cover and cook on Low heat setting for 3½ to 4½ hours or until macaroni is tender.

Sweet Potato Turkey Bowl

Prep 15 minutes **Cook** 3½ to 4½ hours (Low) **Makes** 6 servings

Canola oil cooking spray

3¼ cups chicken broth

2 packets (5 ounces each) yellow saffron rice

2 tablespoons lemon juice

2 teaspoons chopped garlic

2 pounds boneless skinless turkey breast, cut into bite-size pieces

1 tablespoon lemon-and-herb seasoning

1 can (15-ounce) apricot halves in juice, drained

1 bag (8-ounce) cut sweet potatoes

1 cup frozen pepper strips

1 small red onion, chopped

⅓ cup chopped pitted dates

2 teaspoons garam masala

1 teaspoon ground ginger

1. Coat a 5-quart slow cooker with cooking spray. In prepared slow cooker, stir together chicken broth, rice, lemon juice, and garlic until combined. Sprinkle turkey pieces with lemon-and-herb seasoning; add to slow cooker.

2. In a large bowl, stir together apricot halves, sweet potatoes, pepper strips, onion, dates, garam masala, and ginger until combined. Pour over turkey in slow cooker.

3. Cover and cook on Low heat setting for 3½ to 4½ hours.

4. To serve, ladle into shallow bowls.

Butter Salmon with Leeks

Prep 15 minutes   **Cook** 2 hours (High) + 1½ to 2 hours (Low)   **Makes** 4 servings

¼ cup butter

2 tablespoons extra virgin olive oil

3 medium leeks, cut in half lengthwise, cleaned, sliced ¼ inch thick

1½ cups baby carrots, sliced ½ inch thick

¼ cup crumbled cooked bacon

1½ teaspoons vegetable supreme seasoning

2 cans (14.5 ounces each) whole new potatoes, drained

¼ cup vegetable broth

1½ pounds salmon fillet

1½ teaspoons seafood seasoning

2 tablespoons half-and-half

Salt and ground black pepper

1. In a 5-quart slow cooker, combine 2 tablespoons of the butter and the oil. Stir in leeks, carrots, bacon, and vegetable seasoning until combined. Place potatoes on top of vegetables in slow cooker.

2. Cover and cook on High heat setting for 2 hours.

3. Stir in vegetable broth. Turn slow cooker to Low heat setting. Cover and cook for 30 minutes more.

4. Sprinkle salmon with seafood seasoning; place on top of vegetables in slow cooker. Cover and cook for 1 to 1½ hours. Transfer salmon to a serving platter and cut into 4 portions; keep warm.

5. Transfer potatoes to a medium bowl. Add the remaining 2 tablespoons butter and the half-and-half to potatoes. Mash with a potato masher until creamy. Season to taste with salt and pepper.

6. To serve, mound mashed potatoes on serving platter and top with salmon fillets. Arrange leeks and carrots over or alongside salmon. Serve immediately.

Cajun Shrimp and Rice

Prep 10 minutes   **Cook** 3½ to 4 hours (High)   **Makes** 6 servings

3 cups frozen mixed vegetables (corn, carrots, peas, cut green beans)

1 can (15-ounce) black beans, rinsed and drained

1 can (14.5-ounce) diced tomatoes with onions and green peppers

1 box (8-ounce) dirty rice mix

1 can (14-ounce) vegetable broth

1 bottle (8-ounce) clam juice

1 tablespoon chopped garlic

2 teaspoons Cajun spice blend

1 teaspoon seafood seasoning

12 ounces frozen medium cooked shrimp, thawed

1. In a 5-quart slow cooker, stir together mixed vegetables, beans, tomatoes, and rice mix until combined. In a medium bowl, whisk together vegetable broth, clam juice, garlic, Cajun spice blend, and seafood seasoning. Pour into slow cooker; stir until combined.

2. Cover and cook on High heat setting for 3 to 3½ hours.

3. Remove lid. Rice should be slightly wet. Stir in shrimp. Cover and cook for 30 to 40 minutes more or until shrimp is heated through and rice is fully cooked.

Chicken

My Grandma Dicie used to say that there are endless ways to fix chicken and that every piece is good. I might add that there are endless ways to fix chicken in the slow cooker (the bit about every piece being good still stands). Here are lots of delicious ways to cook everyone's favorite bird—and some great recipes for turkey too.

Blue Cheese Chicken

Prep 20 minutes   **Cook** 3 to 3½ hours (Low)   **Makes** 4 servings

2   cups frozen broccoli and cauliflower

1   medium onion, halved then quartered

1   cup chicken broth

⅓   cup butter, softened

2   tablespoons dried chives

2   teaspoons + 1 tablespoon chopped garlic

1   teaspoon lemon juice

4   skinless, boneless chicken breast halves

1   packet garlic-and-herb seasoned coating mix

1   can (10.5-ounce) white sauce

1   cup crumbled blue cheese

1. In a 5-quart slow cooker, combine frozen vegetables and onions. Pour ¼ cup of the chicken broth over vegetables. In a small bowl, stir together butter, chives, 2 teaspoons of the garlic, and the lemon juice until combined; set aside.

2. Place chicken breasts on a cutting board and cover them with plastic wrap. Using a meat mallet, gently pound chicken until ⅓ inch thick. Spread one-fourth of the butter mixture in an even layer on top of each pounded breast. Roll each breast from one end toward the other, enclosing butter mixture. If necessary, secure rolls with wooden toothpicks.

3. Pour coating mix into a pie plate. Roll chicken rolls in coating mix until well coated. Place rolls on top of vegetables in slow cooker.

4. Cover and cook on Low heat setting for 2 hours.

5. In a medium bowl, whisk together the remaining ¾ cup chicken broth, the remaining 1 tablespoon garlic, and white sauce until smooth. Stir in blue cheese. Pour over chicken and vegetables in slow cooker.

6. Cover and cook on Low heat setting for 1 to 1½ hours more. Remove any toothpicks from chicken rolls before serving.

Roasted Pepper Chicken

Prep 10 minutes   **Cook** 3½ to 4½ hours (Low)   **Makes** 6 servings

4   pounds meaty chicken pieces (breast halves, thighs, and drumsticks), skin removed*

1   tablespoon Montreal chicken seasoning

1½   cups frozen chopped onions

1   cup dry red wine

1   jar (8-ounce) roasted red peppers, patted dry and sliced lengthwise

1   cup olive bruschetta topping

1   tablespoon chopped garlic

2   teaspoons fennel seeds

½   cup grated Parmesan cheese (optional)

¼   cup chopped fresh parsley (optional)

1. Sprinkle chicken with chicken seasoning; place in a 5-quart slow cooker. In a medium bowl, stir together onions, wine, roasted peppers, bruschetta topping, garlic, and fennel seeds until combined; pour over chicken in slow cooker.

2. Cover and cook on Low heat setting for 3½ to 4½ hours. Sprinkle with Parmesan and parsley (optional).

***Note:** To prepare chicken with skin on, season the chicken pieces and dredge in flour to coat lightly. In a large skillet, over medium-high heat, brown chicken in 2 to 3 tablespoons oil.

Creamy Cheesy Chicken

Prep 15 minutes   **Cook** 4 to 5 hours (Low)   **Makes** 6 servings

2   pounds baby white creamer potatoes, cut into ½-inch slices

8   ounces processed cheese, sliced

6   boneless, skinless chicken breasts

2   tablespoons Montreal chicken seasoning

1   can (10.75-ounce) condensed cream of potato soup, *Campbell's®*

¾   cup crumbled cooked bacon

½   cup frozen chopped onions

1   tablespoon chopped fresh chives (plus more for garnish, [optional])

1   teaspoon chopped garlic

1. In a 5-quart slow cooker, layer potato and cheese slices. Sprinkle chicken breasts with chicken seasoning. Place on top of potatoes and cheese in slow cooker.

2. In a large bowl, stir together potato soup, bacon, onions, chives, and garlic until combined. Pour over chicken and potatoes in slow cooker.

3. Cover and cook on Low heat setting for 4 to 5 hours. Sprinkle with additional chopped chives (optional).

Copacabana Chicken

Prep 20 minutes   **Cook** 3½ to 4½ hours (Low)   **Makes** 4 servings

1½ cups frozen chopped green peppers

1 can (15-ounce) black beans, rinsed and drained

1 can (14.5-ounce) diced tomatoes with garlic and green onions

1 large onion, quartered

4 whole peeled garlic cloves

2 teaspoons dried oregano

1 teaspoon ground cumin

Salt and ground black pepper

4 chicken leg quarters, skin removed*

1 can (10.75-ounce) condensed cream of chicken soup, Campbell's®

¼ cup key lime juice

3 tablespoons orange juice concentrate, thawed

2 bay leaves

1. In a 5-quart slow cooker, stir together green peppers, black beans, tomatoes, onion, and garlic until combined. In a small bowl, stir together oregano, cumin, and salt and pepper to taste. Sprinkle chicken quarters with oregano mixture. Place chicken on top of vegetables in slow cooker.

2. In a medium bowl, whisk together chicken soup, lime juice, and orange juice concentrate until combined. Pour over chicken and vegetables in slow cooker. Place bay leaves on top.

3. Cover and cook on Low heat setting for 3½ to 4½ hours. Remove and discard bay leaves.

*Note: To prepare chicken with skin on, season chicken as directed and place on a foil-lined baking sheet. Broil 4 to 6 inches from heat for 8 to 10 minutes or until skin begins to crisp, turning once. Place chicken on top of vegetables in slow cooker.

Chicken Mushroom Cacciatore

Prep 15 minutes   **Cook** 4 to 6 hours (Low)   **Makes** 6 servings

2   **fennel bulbs, trimmed, thinly sliced lengthwise through the root end**

1   **package (8-ounce) sliced fresh brown mushrooms**

4   **pounds meaty chicken pieces (breast halves, thighs, and drumsticks), skin removed***

1   **tablespoon Montreal chicken seasoning**

1   **can (28-ounce) diced tomatoes**

1½   **cups frozen chopped onions**

1   **cup red wine**

2   **tablespoons chopped garlic**

1   **tablespoon dried Italian seasoning**

¼   **cup prepared pesto**

1. In a 5-quart slow cooker, combine fennel and mushrooms. Sprinkle chicken with chicken seasoning; place on vegetables in slow cooker. In a large bowl, stir together tomatoes, onions, wine, garlic, and Italian seasoning until combined. Pour over chicken in slow cooker.

2. Cover and cook on Low heat setting for 4 to 6 hours.

3. Transfer chicken to a serving platter. Stir pesto into slow cooker. Spoon fennel mixture into serving bowls and serve with chicken.

***Note:** To prepare chicken with skin on, season the chicken pieces and dredge in flour to coat lightly. In a large skillet, brown chicken in 2 to 3 tablespoons oil over medium-high heat.

Gravy-Smothered Chicken

Prep 10 minutes   **Cook** 3 to 4 hours (Low)   **Makes** 4 servings

3   **pounds meaty chicken pieces (breast halves, thighs, and drumsticks)**

   Salt and ground black pepper

2   **jars (12 ounces each) chicken gravy**

1   **package (8-ounce) sliced fresh mushrooms**

1   **cup frozen seasoning blend**

2   **tablespoons chopped garlic**

2   **teaspoons chicken seasoning**

1. Sprinkle chicken with salt and pepper; place in a 5-quart slow cooker. In a large bowl, stir together gravy, mushrooms, seasoning blend, garlic, and chicken seasoning until combined. Pour over chicken in slow cooker.

2. Cover and cook on Low heat setting for 3 to 4 hours.

3. Remove chicken from slow cooker. Serve hot.

Mandarin Turkey Tenderloin

Prep 10 minutes   **Cook** 3½ to 4½ hours (Low)   **Stand** 10 minutes   **Makes** 4 servings

1	bag (16-ounce) frozen stir-fry vegetables
2	pounds turkey tenderloins
2	tablespoons onion soup mix
1	teaspoon ground ginger
1	can (11-ounce) mandarin orange segments, drained
1	cup sesame ginger marinade
½	cup chicken broth
½	teaspoon red pepper flakes
1	tablespoon sesame seeds, toasted
1	scallion (green onion), sliced
	Hot cooked white or brown rice

1. Place vegetables in a 4- to 5-quart slow cooker. Sprinkle all sides of tenderloins with onion soup mix and ginger. Place on top of vegetables in slow cooker. Top turkey with mandarin orange segments.

2. In a small bowl, stir together marinade, chicken broth, and red pepper flakes until combined. Pour over turkey in slow cooker.

3. Cover and cook on Low heat setting for 3½ to 4½ hours.

4. Transfer turkey to a cutting board; let rest for 10 minutes before slicing. Serve sliced turkey with vegetables and mandarin oranges. Sprinkle with toasted sesame seeds and sliced scallion. Serve with hot cooked rice.

Zesty Turkey with Artichokes

Prep 15 minutes   **Cook** 4 to 5 hours (Low)   **Makes** 6 servings

2   cups frozen sliced carrots

1   can (14.5-ounce) diced tomatoes, cut up

1   can (13.75-ounce) quartered artichoke hearts, drained

1   medium onion, chopped

¾   cup sliced black olives

8   whole peeled garlic cloves

1   boneless skinless turkey breast half

     Salt and ground black pepper

1   pound linguica sausage links, sliced

¾   cup reduced-sodium chicken broth

1   can (6-ounce) tomato paste

¼   cup white wine

1   tablespoon dried oregano

1. In a 5-quart slow cooker, stir together carrots, tomatoes, artichoke hearts, onions, olives, and garlic until combined. Sprinkle turkey with salt and pepper to taste. Place turkey and sausage on top of vegetables in slow cooker.

2. In a medium bowl, whisk together chicken broth, tomato paste, wine, and oregano; pour over turkey in slow cooker.

3. Cover and cook on Low heat setting for 4 to 5 hours.

Turkey Cassoulet

Prep 25 minutes   **Cook** 5 to 6 hours (Low) + 30 to 45 minutes (Low)   **Makes** 6 servings

6   slices bacon

2   turkey drumsticks

     Salt and ground black pepper

2   cans (15 ounces each) Great Northern beans, rinsed and drained

1   pound turkey kielbasa sausage, sliced

1   can (14.5-ounce) petite-cut diced tomatoes with garlic and olive oil

½   container (14-ounce) celery and carrot sticks, finely chopped

1   cup frozen chopped onions

1   large leek, halved lengthwise, cleaned, and sliced

1   tablespoon chopped garlic

2   teaspoons herbes de Provence

2   bay leaves

¾   cup crushed seasoned croutons

1. In a large skillet, over medium-high heat, cook bacon until crispy, turning frequently. Drain on paper towels; reserve bacon drippings in skillet. Chop bacon and place in a 5-quart slow cooker.

2. Sprinkle turkey drumsticks with salt and pepper. In skillet with reserved bacon grease, over medium-high heat, cook drumsticks until skin is crisp. Transfer drumsticks to slow cooker.

3. Add beans, kielbasa, tomatoes, celery and carrots, onions, leek, garlic, and herbes de Provence to slow cooker; stir until combined. Place bay leaves on top.

4. Cover and cook on Low heat setting for 5 to 6 hours.

5. Remove and discard bay leaves. Remove drumsticks from slow cooker. Carefully remove meat from drumsticks; return meat to slow cooker. Sprinkle crushed croutons over top. Cook, uncovered, on Low heat setting for 30 to 45 minutes more.

Turkey Divan

Prep 15 minutes   **Cook** 3 to 4 hours (Low)   **Makes** 6 servings

Canola oil cooking spray

6   turkey breast cutlets, cut into bite-size pieces

1   tablespoon lemon-and-herb seasoning

2   boxes (10 ounces each) frozen chopped broccoli

1   cup frozen seasoning blend

1   can (10.75-ounce) condensed cream of broccoli soup, *Campbell's*®

1   can (10.5-ounce) white sauce

1½   cups shredded sharp cheddar cheese

1   cup shredded Parmesan cheese

¼   cup mayonnaise

1   teaspoon garlic powder

½   teaspoon curry powder

1   cup crushed potato chips

Hot cooked noodles or rice (optional)

1. Coat a 4-quart slow cooker with cooking spray. Sprinkle turkey pieces with lemon-and-herb seasoning; place in slow cooker. Add broccoli and seasoning blend.

2. In a large bowl, whisk together broccoli soup, white sauce, cheddar cheese, seasoning blend, Parmesan cheese, mayonnaise, garlic powder, and curry powder until combined. Pour over chicken and broccoli in slow cooker; stir to combine.

3. Cover and cook on Low heat setting 3 to 4 hours.

4. Serve warm with crushed potato chips over top. Serve over cooked noodles or rice (optional).

Turkey Stroganoff

Prep 15 minutes   **Cook** 3 to 4 hours (Low) + 30 minutes (High)   **Makes** 6 servings

1½   cups frozen chopped onions

1   package (8-ounce) sliced fresh white mushrooms

1   package (8-ounce) sliced fresh baby portobello mushrooms

1   tablespoon chopped garlic

2   pounds turkey breast tenders, cut into 1-inch pieces

2   teaspoons poultry seasoning

      Salt and ground black pepper

2   jars (12 ounces each) mushroom gravy

⅓   cup dry sherry

1   cup sour cream

      Hot cooked wide egg noodles (optional)

      Chopped fresh flat-leaf parsley (optional)

1. In a 5-quart slow cooker, stir together onions, all mushrooms, and garlic until combined. Sprinkle turkey with poultry seasoning and salt and pepper to taste. Place on mushrooms in slow cooker.

2. In a medium bowl, whisk together gravy and sherry until combined. Pour over turkey in slow cooker.

3. Cover and cook on Low heat setting for 3 to 4 hours.

4. Stir in sour cream. Turn slow cooker to High heat setting and cook for 30 minutes more. Serve stroganoff over hot cooked egg noodles (optional) and sprinkle with parsley (optional).

Pepper Pineapple Turkey Ham

Prep 10 minutes   **Cook** 4 to 5 hours (Low)   **Stand** 10 minutes   **Makes** 4 servings

1	medium onion, sliced
2	cups frozen pepper strips
1	2-pound turkey ham
2	teaspoons seasoned pepper
1	can (20-ounce) pineapple chunks
4	whole garlic cloves
½	cup packed brown sugar

1. In a 4- to 5-quart slow cooker, combine onion slices and peppers. Sprinkle all sides of turkey ham with seasoned pepper. Place on top of vegetables in slow cooker. Add pineapple chunks and garlic cloves. Sprinkle brown sugar over top.

2. Cover and cook on Low heat setting for 4 to 5 hours.

3. Transfer turkey ham to a cutting board; let rest for 10 minutes before slicing. Place ham on serving platter and pour accumulated juices over slices. Serve with pineapples, peppers, and onion slices.

SERVING IDEA: Serve this with premade mashed potatoes and warmed Hawaiian sweet rolls.

Beef

Some of the tastiest cuts of beef are the most economical (see the guide on page 8 for the best buys). Sit down to a hearty dinner of smoky Cappuccino Pot Roast, fragrant Beef Mole Stew, or buttery Teriyaki Short Ribs with Spicy Mash and you'll feel as rich as royalty!

Irish Pub Brisket

Prep 15 minutes   **Cook** 8 hours (Low) or 4 hours (High)   **Makes** 8 servings

1   pound carrots (about 5 medium),
     cut into 2- to 3-inch pieces

1   3-pound beef brisket, trimmed

1½   teaspoons salt

2   cups stout-style beer

3   tablespoons mixed pickling spice

1   tablespoon prepared horseradish

1   tablespoon chopped garlic

2   teaspoons salt

8   small new potatoes, unpeeled

1   small green cabbage, cored and
     cut into 8 wedges

     Stone-ground mustard, for serving

     Horseradish, for serving

1. Place carrots in a 6-quart slow cooker. Rub brisket with salt. Place brisket on top of carrots in slow cooker. (If necessary, cut brisket to fit.) In a medium bowl, stir together beer, pickling spice, horseradish, garlic, and salt. Pour over brisket in slow cooker. Place potatoes around brisket and place the cabbage on top, pressing down firmly.

2. Cover and cook on Low heat setting for 8 hours or on High heat setting for 4 hours.

3. Serve brisket with stone-ground mustard and horseradish.

Sweet Tea Brisket

Prep 15 minutes **Cook** 8 to 10 hours (Low) **Makes** 6 servings

2 large sweet onions, thickly sliced

2 lemons, sliced

1 3-pound beef brisket, trimmed

¼ cup Worcestershire sauce

1 tablespoon Montreal steak seasoning

2 packets beefy onion soup mix

1½ cups honey-brown sugar barbecue sauce

1 cup sweetened lemon-flavored tea

½ cup honey mustard

1. In a 6-quart slow cooker, combine sliced onions and lemons. Sprinkle brisket with Worcestershire sauce and steak seasoning. Place brisket in slow cooker. (If necessary, cut brisket to fit.) Sprinkle with onion soup mix.

2. In a medium bowl, whisk together barbecue sauce, tea, and honey mustard; pour over brisket in slow cooker.

3. Cover and cook on Low heat setting for 8 to 10 hours.

4. Transfer brisket to a cutting board; let rest for 10 minutes before slicing. Using a wire mesh strainer, stain sauce. Serve sauce with brisket.

BBQ Beef Sliders
with Sesame Slaw

Prep 15 minutes   **Cook** 8 to 10 hours (Low)   **Stand** 10 minutes   **Makes** 12 servings

FOR BRISKET:

1	4-pound beef brisket, trimmed
2	packages (1.6 ounces each) slow cooker **BBQ** pulled pork seasoning
1	bottle (18-ounce) barbecue sauce
1	cup unsweetened natural applesauce
1	cup apple cider
1	tablespoon prepared horseradish
1	tablespoon chopped garlic
1	tablespoon ginger spice blend

FOR COLESLAW:

1	bag (16-ounce) tri-color coleslaw mix
¾	cup slaw dressing
2	tablespoons sesame seeds, toasted
36	dinner rolls, split almost all the way through

1. For brisket, rub the brisket with both packages of pulled pork seasoning; set aside. In a 6-quart slow cooker, stir together barbecue sauce, applesauce, apple cider, horseradish, garlic, and ginger until combined. Add brisket, turning several times to coat. (If necessary, cut brisket to fit.)

2. Cover and cook on Low heat setting for 8 to 10 hours.

3. Transfer brisket to a platter; let rest for 10 minutes. Pour cooking liquid into a medium saucepan; simmer over medium heat until sauce is reduced by at least half and is syrupy. Taste sauce for seasoning, adding *salt, pepper,* or more horseradish. While sauce is reducing, use two forks to shred brisket. Toss brisket with the sauce.

4. For coleslaw, in a medium bowl, toss the coleslaw mix with slaw dressing and sesame seeds. Cover and refrigerate for up to 1 day.

5. To serve, open a dinner roll and put some shredded brisket on it. Top the brisket with a heaping forkful of coleslaw. Serve immediately.

Cappuccino Pot Roast

Prep 15 minutes   **Cook** 8 to 10 hours (Low)   **Makes** 10 servings

1	**4-pound beef chuck roast, trimmed**
½	**teaspoon salt**
	Coarsely ground pepper
1	**package (16-ounce) baby carrots**
2	**large yellow onions, coarsely chopped**
¼	**cup sliced jalapeños**
2	**tablespoons chopped garlic**
1	**cup strong-brewed coffee**
1	**packet (1.5-ounce) beef stew mix**
2	**tablespoon balsamic vinegar**
2	**cubes chipotle bouillon cubes, crumbled**
1	**bay leaf, crumbled**
1	**container (8-ounce) sour cream**

1. Sprinkle roast with salt and pepper to taste; set aside. In a 6-quart slow cooker, combine carrots, onions, jalapeños, and garlic. Place roast on vegetables in slow cooker.

2. In a medium bowl, stir together coffee, beef stew mix, vinegar, bouillon cubes, and bay leaf until combined. Pour over roast in slow cooker.

3. Cover and cook on Low heat setting for 8 to 10 hours.

4. Transfer roast to a cutting board; let rest for 10 minutes before slicing. Using a slotted spoon, transfer vegetables to a serving platter. Add sliced roast to platter. Using a wire mesh strainer, strain sauce. Stir sour cream into sauce; serve with roast and vegetables.

Steak with Creamy Crawfish Sauce

Prep 25 minutes   **Cook** 7 to 8 hours (Low)   **Makes** 4 servings

FOR STEAK AND STUFFING:

1	2-pound flank steak
2	teaspoons Cajun seasoning blend
8	ounces Andouille sausage, casing removed and crumbled or chopped
2	tablespoons chopped pimientos
1	tablespoon tomato paste
1	teaspoon prepared horseradish
1	package (6-ounce) savory herb stuffing mix
½	cup chicken broth
¼	cup water

FOR CRAWFISH SAUCE:

4	tablespoons butter
½	cup minced onion
½	cup minced red bell pepper
½	cup minced celery
1½	cups half-and-half
1	packet (1.6-ounce) garlic and herb sauce mix
2	teaspoons Cajun seasoning blend
1	bag (8-ounce) frozen crawfish, thawed
1	jar (4.5-ounce) sliced mushrooms, drained
2	tablespoons chopped fresh parsley

1. Lay the steak out flat; with a sharp knife, lightly score meat diagonally to the grain of the meat, about 1 inch apart and ¼ inch deep. Pound flat with a meat mallet. Sprinkle both sides with Cajun seasoning. Set aside.

2. In a medium skillet, over high heat, cook and stir sausage for 3 minutes. Reduce heat to medium and add pimientos. Stir in tomato paste and horseradish. Pour the stuffing mix over all and drizzle with the broth; stir well to combine. Stuffing should be moist but not runny.

3. Spoon stuffing mixture down the middle of unscored side of flank steak. Fold short ends over and overlap long sides to enclose stuffing. Secure with skewers or tie with 100-percent-cotton kitchen string. Place steak roll on metal rack or trivet in a 5-quart slow cooker. Add water to slow cooker.

4. Cover and cook on Low heat setting for 7 to 8 hours. When meat is done, pour off any liquids that have accumulated in the cooker, reserving ½ cup for the sauce.

5. For crawfish sauce, in a medium skillet over medium-high heat, melt the butter. Add the onions, bell pepper, and celery; cook and stir until the vegetables are tender, about 5 minutes. Combine the half-and-half and sauce mix and add to cooked vegetables; strain in the ½ cup reserved pot juices. Add seasoning blend and bring to a boil. Add crawfish and mushrooms; reduce heat to medium. Continue to cook, stirring constantly, until the pan reaches a simmer, stirring until thick. Stir in the parsley.

6. Transfer steak roll to a cutting board; remove skewers or string and slice roll. Serve sauce with steak.

Beef Mole Stew

Prep 15 minutes   **Cook** 4 to 6 hours (High)   **Makes** 4 servings

2 pounds beef stew meat, cut into bite-size pieces

1 cup frozen chopped onions

2 tablespoons Mexican seasoning

4 cups beef broth

¼ cup sesame seeds

2 tablespoons diced jalapeños

2 tablespoons tomato paste

1 tablespoon chopped garlic

1 teaspoon dried Mexican oregano

¼ teaspoon ancho chile powder

½ teaspoon ground cinnamon

2 ounces dark chocolate, chopped

Slivered almonds, toasted (optional)

Crumbled queso fresco (optional)

Warm flour tortillas or hot cooked Mexican rice (optional)

1. In a 4-quart slow cooker, combine stew meat and onions. Sprinkle with Mexican seasoning. In a large bowl, whisk together beef broth, sesame seeds, jalapeños, tomato paste, garlic, oregano, chile powder, and cinnamon until combined. Pour into slow cooker; stir to combine.

2. Cover and cook on High heat setting for 4 to 6 hours. During the last hour of cooking, add chopped chocolate to slow cooker.

3. Stir before serving. Sprinkle with slivered almonds and queso fresco (optional). Serve beef mole with warm tortillas or over hot cooked Mexican rice (optional).

Teriyaki Short Ribs
with Spicy Mash

Prep 20 minutes **Cook** 8 to 10 hours (Low) **Makes** 4 servings

FOR SHORT RIBS:

1	cup teriyaki sauce
1	cup hoisin sauce
½	cup beef broth
½	teaspoon whole black peppercorns
12	beef short ribs

FOR POTATOES:

1	package (24-ounce) frozen garlic-seasoned mashed potatoes
⅓	cup warm milk
2	tablespoons unsalted butter, cut into pieces
1½	teaspoons Asian five-spice blend
2	scallions (green onions), sliced

1. For short ribs, in a medium bowl, stir together teriyaki sauce, hoisin sauce, beef broth, and peppercorns. Dip ribs in sauce to coat; place in a 5-quart slow cooker, bone sides down. Pour remaining sauce over ribs in slow cooker.

2. Cover and cook on Low heat setting for 8 to 10 hours.

3. Transfer short ribs to a serving platter; keep warm. Skim off any fat from the top of sauce. Pour sauce into medium saucepan. Simmer over medium-high heat until sauce is thickened. Reserve ⅓ cup sauce for potatoes.

4. For potatoes, microwave according to package directions. Transfer potatoes to a large bowl. Add reserved ⅓ cup sauce, the warm milk, butter, and five-spice blend. Mash to desired consistency. Sprinkle with scallions. Serve ribs with mashed potatoes and sauce.

Venetian Veal Chops

Prep 15 minutes   **Cook** 4 to 5 hours (Low)   **Makes** 4 servings

1 ½   cups baby carrots

3   turnips, quartered and sliced

1   can (14.5-ounce) diced tomatoes

4   veal loin chops

1   teaspoon celery salt

¼   teaspoon ground black pepper

1   can (10.75-ounce) condensed cream of onion soup, *Campbell's*®

½   cup beef broth

2 ½   tablespoons prepared horseradish

1   tablespoon Worcestershire sauce

Fresh flat-leaf parsley sprigs (optional)

1. In a 5-quart slow cooker, stir together carrots, turnips, and tomatoes until combined. Sprinkle veal chops with celery salt and pepper. Place on top of vegetables in slow cooker.

2. In a medium bowl, whisk together onion soup, beef broth, horseradish, and Worcestershire sauce until combined. Pour over veal in slow cooker.

3. Cover and cook on Low heat setting for 4 to 5 hours.

4. Using a wire mesh strainer, strain cooking juices. Skim off any fat from the top of the juices. Serve chops with vegetables and cooking juices. Garnish with parsley (optional).

Lemon Herbed Veal Roast

Prep 10 minutes   **Cook** 6 to 7 hours (Low)   **Stand** 10 minutes   **Makes** 4 servings

1	pound fingerling potatoes, cut in half
1	can (15-ounce) diced tomatoes, drained
1	cup frozen pepper strips
1	cup frozen chopped onions
1	2½-pound boneless veal shoulder roast
2	teaspoons lemon-and-herb seasoning
1	can (14-ounce) chicken broth
1	jar (10-ounce) garlic-stuffed olives, drained, cut in half
2	tablespoons capers

1. In a 5-quart slow cooker, stir together potatoes, tomatoes, pepper strips, and onions. Sprinkle veal shoulder with lemon-and-herb seasoning. Place on top of vegetables in slow cooker. Pour chicken broth over veal shoulder. Top with olives and capers.

2. Cover and cook on Low heat setting for 6 to 7 hours.

3. Transfer roast to a cutting board; let rest for 10 minutes before slicing. Serve sliced veal with vegetables, olives, capers, and cooking juices.

Garlic Wine Veal Shanks

Prep 15 minutes   **Cook** 7 to 8 hours (Low)   **Makes** 4 servings

VEAL SHANKS:

2	cans (14.5 ounces each) whole new potatoes, drained
2	cups frozen pearl onions
1	can (14.5-ounce) diced tomatoes with roasted garlic
4	center-cut veal shanks
1	can (10.75-ounce) condensed cream of celery soup, *Campbell's*®
½	cup chicken broth
½	cup dry white wine
½	teaspoon ground nutmeg

GREMOLATA:

¼	cup finely chopped fresh flat-leaf parsley
1	tablespoon lemon zest
1½	teaspoons chopped garlic

1. For veal shanks, in a 5-quart slow cooker, stir together potatoes, onions, and tomatoes until combined. Place veal shanks on top of vegetables in slow cooker. In a medium bowl, whisk together celery soup, chicken broth, wine, and nutmeg until combined. Pour over veal shanks in slow cooker.

2. Cover and cook on Low heat setting for 7 to 8 hours.

3. For gremolata, in a small bowl, stir together chopped parsley, lemon zest, and garlic until combined.

4. Transfer veal shanks to serving platter. Using a wire mesh strainer, strain cooking juices. Skim off any fat from the top of cooking juices. Serve veal shanks with vegetables and cooking juices. Sprinkle with gremolata just before serving.

Index

Sandra Lee Semi-Homemade Cookbook Series

Collect all of these smartly helpful, time-saving, and beautiful books by New York Times best-selling author and Food Network star, Sandra Lee.

sandralee.com

Sandra Lee has a passion for simple solutions that create dramatic results in all areas of home life. For exclusive recipes, time- and money-saving tips and tricks to make your home life easier, better and more enjoyable, log on to www.SandraLee.com. Sign up for the Semi-Homemaker's online club to receive free newsletters filled with fabulous recipes and great entertaining at-home ideas.

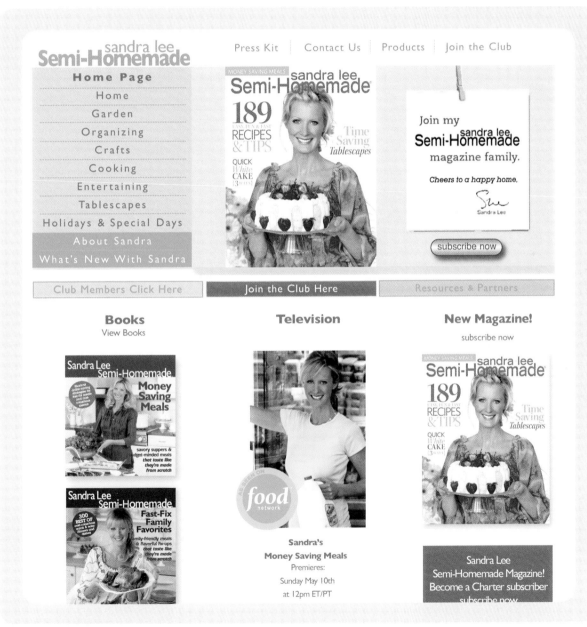

Go to SandraLee.com or Semihomemade.com

Making life easier, better, and more enjoyable